PORTIONS *of* LIGHT

CHAYENU

PORTIONS OF LIGHT
TEACHINGS FROM THE HOLY BAAL SHEM TOV
ON TORAH AND FESTIVALS

Copyright © 2020 by
CHAYENU
info@chayenu.org | www.chayenu.org

Original Hebrew text copyright ©
Kehot Publication Society

First Printing—February 2020

Published by
KEHOT PUBLICATION SOCIETY
770 Eastern Parkway / Brooklyn, New York 11213
(718) 774-4000 / FAX (718) 774-2718
editor@kehot.com / www.kehot.org

ORDER DEPARTMENT:
291 Kingston Avenue / Brooklyn, New York 11213
(718) 778-0226 / FAX (718) 778-4148
www.kehot.com

1 3 5 7 9 10 8 6 4 2

ISBN 978-0-8266-0881-9

Printed in the United States of America

Cover Design: Spotlight – Brooklyn, NY

PORTIONS
of LIGHT

מלוקט מספר כתר שם טוב

Teachings From the Holy Baal Shem Tov
On Torah and Festivals

THIS EDITION OF KETER SHEM TOV IS
JOYOUSLY DEDICATED IN HONOR OF

RICK & LOTTY SCHULLER
חיים וחיה שולער שי׳

*In celebration of their 50th wedding anniversary and in gratitude
for their boundless love and generosity bestowed upon their
children, grandchildren, great grandchildren, and Klal Yisrael*

BY THEIR FAMILY

שמעון ויעל דוידה שי׳ — **Shimon & Yael Davidah**
ר׳ בנימין מיכאל שי׳ — **Rabbi Benjamin Michael**
גבריאל יוסף שי׳ — **Gavriel Yosef**
אליענה אריאלה דבורה שת׳ — **Elianna Ariella Devorah**
זכריה מאיר שי׳ — **Zechariah Meier**
יעקב דובער שי׳ — **Yaacov Dov Ber**
חנה עליה שת׳ — **Chana Alea**

— **Schuller Family** —

ר׳ אברהם חיים ועדינה שי׳ — **Rabbi Avraham Chaim & Adina**
יעקב מאיר שי׳ — **Yakov Meir**

— **Soussan Family** —

אלון ואורלי מינדל יהודית שי׳ — **Alon & Orlie Mindel Yehudis**
נועה לאה שת׳ — **Noa Leah**
יוסף יצחק שי׳ — **Yosef Yitzchak**
חנה רחל שת׳ — **Chana Rochel**
מנחם מענדל שי׳ — **Menachem Mendel**

— **Zak Family** —

AND IN TRIBUTE TO

ר׳ נפתלי הערץ שי׳ — **Rabbi Naftoli Hertz Estulin**
for health and happiness with Mashiach now

Contents

Preface

On Rosh Hashanah eve, 5507 (1746), the Baʾal Shem Tov's soul made a heavenly journey. No, he did not pass away. He had what is known as *aliyat haneshamah* (a soul ascent), whereby he made a visit to the supernal realm, the world of souls.

Accompanied by his spirit-mentor , Achiyah Hashiloni, he came to the chamber of the soul of Mashiach, where he witnessed Mashiach's soul teaching the deepest secrets of Torah to the sages of the Talmud and other Jewish leaders (of their time). He witnessed incredible joy and wondered about its cause.

In a letter penned to his brother-in-law, R. Gershon Kitover (who had moved to the Holy Land), the Baʾal Shem Tov describes the scene and the following exchange.

"I asked the (soul of) Mashiach: 'When will the master (finally) come?!'"

"Mashiach replied: '...When your wellsprings will be spread outward...'"

These words of Mashiach are understood to mean that when the teachings of the Baʾal Shem Tov—his new path of Chasidism and Chasidic teaching—will be disseminated to the widest and furthest arena, then the world will be ready for the ultimate redemption.

It was with the guidance of this teaching that Chayenu embarked on the project of translating teachings of the Ba'al Shem Tov into English. What better way to push the teachings of the Ba'al Shem Tov more "outward" than translating it from Hebrew to English and expanding the scope of students learning his teachings from the inner circle of Hebrew students to the English-speaking crowd that would not otherwise have access to these teachings.

There is yet another benefit of translating the teachings of Chasidus, because it has a quality that speaks to the soul. When a person learns a section of Talmud, he learns G-d's laws, but it is His laws as they pertain to mundane and material matters. Chasidut is a Divine teaching that speaks of the soul and to the soul. This is especially true of the Ba'al Shem Tov, who was revealed in order to revive the soul of the Jewish people, who were suffering through spiritual and physical hardship at the hands of the Sabbatian movement and pogroms.

The Ba'al Shem Tov's teachings span many ideas and explain numerous biblical verses and teachings of the sages, which can sometimes be cumbersome for someone who is trying to understand his words. Therefore, we chose to focus on a specific point within a larger teaching and extrapolate a "bite-size" message so that a novice to Chasidic in-depth analysis will also be able to follow the message, take it to heart, and live with it.

The Ba'al Shem tov himself didn't transcribe his teachings; rather, they were collected and published by some of his students and followers. Two of the more famous works are *Keter Shem Tov* (Zalkva, 1794) and *Tzava'at Harivash* (Zalkva, c. 1792). More recently, in 1973, Kehot Publication Society published a new edition of *Keter Shem Tov*, with an addendum that includes teachings of the Ba'al Shem Tov that were transmitted by the Chabad Rebbes in their talks and discourses.

The teachings of the Ba'al Shem Tov published in Chayenu were culled from this new print of *Keter Shem Tov*.

Every work begins with an idea. This book started because of the "one minute of Torah" podcast of **Rabbi Moshe Levin** of Bais Bezalel Chabad, which is located in the Pico-Robertson neighborhood of Los Angeles.

One couple who regularly listen to this class were so inspired by the teachings of the Ba'al Shem Tov that they reached out to Rabbi Levin to make a series of recordings just about the Ba'al Shem Tov's teachings.

One woman attending that class was so inspired that she reached out to the Chayenu editors, suggesting the teachings of the Ba'al Shem Tov become a section in Chayenu. The rest is history.

Thank you, **Mrs. Ilana Yakovelev**, for having the foresight in seeing the importance of this project, for making the connection, and for your involvement in this project all the way through from conception to publication. Thank you for your generous support in this work. May you be blessed with much *nachat* and success in all your endeavors.

With the passage of time many Chayenu readers asked how can they access these teachings of the Ba'al Shem Tov—which we have featured each week of the past few years years—in an ongoing, organized way.

That's how the idea for this book was born. It dawned on us that perhaps there is an even wider audience waiting to learn the teachings of the Ba'al Shem Tov; perhaps there is someone who feels that he/she needs the inspiration of the Baʾal Shem Tov more often, or there is a person who is not yet a Chayenu student but is thirsty to drink from the Baʾal Shem Tov's wellsprings. This motivated us to compile the teachings as a book and publish them as a self-standing work.

Portions of Light

In a talk delivered by the Previous Lubavitcher Rebbe, R. Yosef Yizchak, and now printed as a preface to the Kehot edition of *Keter Shem Tov*, the Rebbe said that *Keter Shem Tov* was one of three books that his father, R. Shalom Dov Ber, the fifth Lubavitcher Rebbe, always kept handy. He would read some lines from it before he would have private audiences (*yechidut*) with his followers, before he would pray, and before he would recite the *Shema* before going to bed.

The Previous Rebbe said that it is difficult for him to reveal this information (presumably, because of this being a hidden and personal conduct of his father. Chayenu Ed.), but because of *ahavat Yisrael*, love for a fellow Jew, he cannot withhold this information, which demonstrates the importance of *Keter Shem Tov*, and the importance of learning from it often.

The Previous Rebbe concludes: "It is important and proper that Chasidim should have in their possession these three books (*Keter Shem Tov*, *Ohr Hatorah* and *Tanya*).... Study from them as much as one desires, but one should learn from them. Each day, or at least on Shabbat and Jewish festivals, and at designated times."

With this clear message in mind, we have broken up the teachings into the portions of the week, having each "bite-size" teaching, or shall we say "portion" of teaching, associated with the week's Torah portion. Likewise, we have a teaching for each of the Jewish festivals and for the Ethics of our Fathers (Pirkei Avot).

We have added an addendum where selected teachings concerning the recital of *Tehillim* (Psalms) have been translated as well as insight on the importance of *Chitat*, the study of *Chumash*, *Tehillim* and *Tanya*.

In order to keep some of the original words of *Keter Shem Tov* and some of the mystical flavor of the original Hebrew, we have included a few lines in the original Hebrew. While this is not always the entire source text for the English teaching, it stands as a "wellspring" in its own right for those who can understand the original Hebrew.

Chasidut is not meant to remain an intellectual pursuit. It is supposed to stir our souls. Move us. With this in mind, after each teaching, we have added a "focus"—something that can be taken as a practical message from what has just been learned; something that we can contemplate and will change our perspective, and make us more Divine conscious.

For the fluidity of the learning experience and design, we have included many of the sources at the end of the book.

Acknowledgment

No book is published without the collective effort of many individuals. We would like to acknowledge and thank **Rabbi Ya'akov Paley** for translating the teachings from the original Hebrew. **Rabbi Itzick Yarmush** for selecting and editing the teachings. **Rabbi Shmuel Rabin** for his editing and important comments. **Mendy Angyalfi** for his extraordinary design and layout of the book. **Moshe Muchnik** and the team at Spotlight Design for the naming and cover design of the book. And to

Rabbis Yosef Boruch Friedman, Dovid Olidort, and Mendel Laine of Kehot Publication Society for their guidance, and mostly for publishing this work with us. Kehot is the official publishing house of Chasidut Chabad and have allowed us use of these sacred texts in the Chayenu weekly study booklet (and the app), for which we are forever grateful.

Thank you, Rabbis Ari Sollish, Levi Mendelow, Moshe Rubin, and Aryeh Pels, for your invaluable advice and encouragement throughout this project.

Thank you, Rabbi Michoel Goldman, founder and editor-in-chief of Chayenu, for your constant advice and encouragement in all the details of this project.

Thank you, Rabbi Levi Wineberg, who was and is a mentor to many of us on the Chayenu team, for writing the Foreword to this book, where you give historical context, elaborate on the importance and relevance of the Ba'al Shem Tov's teachings, and the effect that Chasidism had on the evolving Jewish lifestyle since its appearance.

We would also like to acknowledge the benefactors of this book, Shimon and Yael Schuller, who saw the great opportunity in furthering the work of spreading the wellsprings of Chasidut outward and are dedicating the book in honor of Rick and Lotty Schuller and in tribute to Rabbi Naftoli Hertz Estulin. May you and all of your families be blessed with *nachat* and success in all your endeavors.

And a final thank you to Rabbi Yossi Pels, executive director of Chayenu, for overseeing this entire project from inception to now, when the book is in your, the reader's, hands.

The Chayenu Team

Foreword

R. Yisrael, son of Eliezer and Sarah, was born in 1698 during a dismal period in Jewish history.

Eastern European Jewry had been devastated twice in the previous half-century. The first blow struck in 1648-9, in a series of Cossack massacres that destroyed hundreds of Jewish communities. The second blow struck a mere fifteen years later: By his apostasy, the infamous false messiah, Shabbetai Zevi, crushed the hopes of tens of thousands for imminent redemption. Thus impoverished, leaderless, communally fragmented, and spiritually hopeless, Jewry was mired in disarray and ignorance, and doubtful of their own value in the eyes of G-d.

R. Yisrael, who came to be known as the Baʾal Shem Tov, was G-d's way of reassuring, encouraging, uplifting, and enlightening His people. He taught the people how much G-d loved them, how much he valued their every good deed, every word of prayer, and their Torah study. Above all, he stressed the greatness of each individual, in that each possessed a G-dly soul that by far eclipsed the greatness of spiritual or scholarly accomplishment. Thereby, he leveled the playing field and breathed hope into the masses, who were at once hated by their non-Jewish neighbors and reviled by the Jewish scholarly elite and the rabbinical preachers, who excoriated them in their sermons.

It was to be expected that the Ba'al Shem Tov's message would meet stiff resistance in the scholarly ranks. They would feel that he was undermining the value of Torah scholarship and undermining the hierarchy in Jewish society by teaching about the value inherent in each individual. Yet, the movement grew exponentially in the twenty-two years of the Ba'al Shem Tov's leadership, from 1738 to 1760.

The Ba'al Shem Tov was able to withstand the opposition thanks to Heavenly reassurance that the propagation of his teachings would, in fact, prepare the way for the Messianic redemption.

Though based in Mezhibuzh, the Ba'al Shem Tov traveled extensively, reaching and teaching the people on their own turf, in the market places and at the trade fairs, in addition to instructing his illustrious pupils in his study hall in Mezhibuzh.

He also attained a reputation as a healer and a fount of blessings, which he achieved through the use of Divine names that have these properties. It was in this sense that he was described as a *Ba'al Shem* "Master of the Name (of G-d)."

When he passed away on Shavuot of 1760, the Ba'al Shem Tov left behind a European Jewry that was energized and hopeful, and a corps of his close students—scholars and saints all—who were ready to take the movement by then known as Chassidut to its next stage of development.

The Ba'al Shem Tov taught in pithy, powerful homilies. Though based on profound mystical teachings, and on Talmudic scholarship, his words were transmitted in simple language, free of scholarly terminology. That way, the average Jew would understand him, and the scholar would appreciate the profundity of his ideas. He did not commit his homilies to writing. The Chassidic texts of the Baʿal Shem Tov are transcriptions by his disciples from the Yiddish vernacular in which they were delivered into biblical Hebrew. While they captured his ideas, they could not transmit the love and the nuances of expression with which the teachings were replete.

For the modern reader, however, lacking the context in which the teachings are set, it may be quite daunting to decipher the meaning of these teachings. Additionally, as the founder of the Chassidic movement, the Baʿal Shem Tov is seen in relation to his successors as "the *sefirah* of *keter*," the "crown," the Divine attribute transcending all the others—which are depicted as the form of man from the head downward.

His teachings are likewise overarching. His soul was the fount of life to all the souls of Israel. The work of his students and successors was to formulate and articulate his transcendental teachings, and to instill the life-energy of the fount into individual souls.

Among the collections of the Baʿal Shem Tov's teachings, the best-known is *Keter Shem Tov* (literally, the Crown of a Good Name). The title is a pun on the Baʿal Shem Tov's title and on the Mishnah in *Avot* that states that this crown is superior to the crowns of Torah, priesthood, and royalty. Many of the qualities described above are present in this anthology of teachings from the *Keter Shem Tov*.

Rabbi Yaakov Paley has skillfully conveyed into lucid and accessible English the allusive, pithy, and often cryptic text of the original—challenging even to the reader fluent in the original Hebrew. He has also provided context and filled in the phrases merely alluded to in the original. The overall result is a flowing and inspiring work.

Credit and our thanks are due to both the writer and the publisher, Rabbi Itzick Yarmush, editor of Chayenu magazine, for bringing this work to the English-speaking public, who are hungry for authentic Chassidut. It is a particular source of *nachat* to me, personally, as this work is the fruit of the collaboration of these two students of mine.

I would urge the reader to seek out in the teachings presented here the themes basic to the Ba'al Shem Tov's thought, such as:

- How a Jew's body and soul are precious to G-d;

- How words and letters have the power to shape our reality;

- How all the spiritual realms are impacted by our words, deeds, and even thoughts.

May G-d grant that this publication further the goal of "spreading the Ba'al Shem Tov's wellsprings abroad," which will lead to the coming of our righteous Mashiach, speedily.

Rabbi Levy Wineberg,
Shliach of the Rebbe to Johannesburg, South Africa

A Day That
Brightens a Year

דֶער אוֹר וְחַיּוּת פוּן חָכְמָה וָואס אִיז מֵאִיר אִין שַׁבָּת בְּרֵאשִׁית וֶוערְט
נִמְשָׁךְ עַל כְּלָלוֹת הַשָּׁנָה, וָואס אַלֶּע טֶעג פוּן שָׁנָה, הֵן דִי יְמֵי הַחוֹל
שַׁבָּת וּמוֹעֲדִים הַכְּלָלִיִּים, הֵן דִי מוֹעֲדִים הַפְּרָטִים פוּן יֶעדֶער יָחִיד,
יוֹם הַכְּנִיסָה לְחֶדֶר, יוֹם הַבַּר מִצְוָה אוּן אַנְדֶערֶע יְמֵי חַיֵּי הָאָדָם
וּמְאוֹרְעוֹתָיו זַיְינֶען זֵיי אַלֶּע מְקַבֵּל פוּן דֶעם שַׁבָּת בְּרֵאשִׁית.

Bereishit bara Elokim – In the beginning G-d created...
(Genesis 1:1).

The word *bereishit* (בראשית) can be read as *bet reishit* (ב
ראשית), "two beginnings." For there is a material *bereishit*, namely,
the beginning of the universe, and there is a Torah *bereishit*, the
start of the Torah.

The purpose of these two beginnings—the world and the
Torah—is *bara Elokim*: The word *bara*, "He created," is related
to the word for clarity, and *Elokim* refers to the G-dliness that
is concealed within creation. *Bara Elokim* means to clarify and
reveal the ultimate purpose of this concealment.

The supernal *sefirot* (Divine attributes) similarly contain two heads: The *sefirah* of *keter* and the *sefirah* of *chochmah*, each of which is referred to as *reishit*, a beginning. However, whereas the *keter*-beginning is concealment, the *chochmah*-beginning is revelation, as in the verse, *The beginning of wisdom is the fear of G-d* (Psalms 111:10).

On Shabbat Bereishit, the light and vitality of *chochmah* shines forth and flows across the entire subsequent year. Each day of the year, be it an ordinary weekday, a Shabbat, a festival, or a private festival celebrated by an individual—such as the day a child is first introduced to *cheder*, the day of his bar mitzvah, and other auspicious occasions or events in his life—receives its light and vitality from Shabbat Bereishit.

Your spiritual conduct on this first Shabbat of the year will directly influence your spiritual performance during the rest of the year.

FOCUS

Your spiritual conduct on this first Shabbat of the year will directly influence your spiritual performance during the rest of the year.

An Ark of Words

אַז מִי אִיז פַארְנוּמֶען מִיט דֶער אַרְבֶּעט אוּן דִי דְאַגֹות פֿוּן פַּרְנָסָה נֶעמֶען
אַרוּם דֶעם מֶענְטשָן אַז עֶר קָאן חָלִילָה פַארְטְרִינְקֶען וֶוערְן, אִיז דִי
עֵצָה אֹויף דֶעם "בֹּא אֶל הַתֵּיבָה", מְדַבֵּק זַיין זִיךְ אִין דִי וֶוערְטֶער פֿוּן
תְּפִלָּה וֶוֹאם מִי דַאוְונְט אוּן דִי וֶוערְטֶער פֿוּן תֹּורָה וֶוֹאם מִי לֶערְנְט.

Enter the ark, you and all your household! (Genesis 7:1).

Our souls enter this world on spiritual missions, but we
find ourselves preoccupied with earning a livelihood in order to
sustain our households through the toil of our hands. If we allow
ourselves to become obsessed with our work and driven by
the worries of earning a livelihood, we can drown in mundane
pursuits.

Our solution is contained in the above verse: *Enter the ark!*
The Hebrew word for ark—*teivah*—also means a word. If we
are beset with a flood of mundane concerns, we must enter the
sacred words, so that when we pray, we enter within and attach
ourselves to the very letters of our prayers. When we study, we
must enter within and attach ourselves to the sacred letters of
the Torah.

In the merit of our attachment to the words of prayer and study, we will be granted a spiritual salvation that parallels Noah's physical salvation, which included *his sons and his wife and his sons' wives* (ibid., v. 7). Our families will enter the *teivah* along with us, because Heaven will ensure that all their needs are met.

FOCUS

You have a spiritual "safe space." It is the words of prayer and Torah study.

Growth Through Facing Evil

הַיִּחוּד הָאֲמִתִּי הִיא הַשְּׁכִינָה, וְאֵיךְ כּוֹלֶלֶת ב׳ הֲפָכִים בְּנוֹשֵׂא אֶחָד,
טוֹב וָרָע שֶׁהֵם ב׳ הֲפָכִים, וְהִיא הַיִּחוּד, אֲבָל בֶּאֱמֶת אָתֵי שַׁפִּיר,
כִּי הָרָע הוּא כְּסֵא לְהַטּוֹב... אוֹ עַל יְדֵי שֶׁרוֹאֶה מַעֲשֵׂי הָרְשָׁעִים
יֵשׁ לוֹ הֲנָאָה שֶׁהוּא צַדִּיק וְיֵשׁ לוֹ הֲנָאָה וְתַעֲנוּג עַל יְדֵי הָרַע.

How can the Divine Presence maintain a state of perfect
unity while simultaneously encompassing everything—
including the conflicting extremes of good and evil?

The truth is that evil serves goodness. For example, when
a righteous person witnesses evil, he rejoices that he is not an
evildoer. The evil thereby brings him to a greater appreciation
for his life of Divinity, to the extent that we can almost say it is
elevated through his sacred delight.

When a soul of *atzilut* (the loftiest of the spiritual realms)
descends into this world and sees humans belittling the honor
of the King of the universe, it is grieved at the degradation, but
it is subsequently delighted that it is not counted among such
people.

G-d said to Abram (Genesis 12:1)—the Jewish soul. *Go from your land*—from *atzilut* to *beriah* (the next of the spiritual realms). *From your birthplace*—from *beriah* to *yetzirah*. *From your father's house*—from *yetzirah* to *asiyah* (this physical world), which is *the land that I will show you*—where I will show you the deeds of mortals who belittle My honor.

Abram went as G-d said to him...and there was hunger in the land (Ibid., verses 4 and 10), meaning that he observed the people's lack of belief in G-d. *Abram descended to Egypt [Mitzrayim]* (Ibid., v. 10), meaning that he was pained [*meitzar*]. *Abram ascended from Egypt* (Ibid., 13:1), experiencing far greater delight in his Divine service by contemplating his good fortune at not being like them.

FOCUS

Even negative experiences are Divinely ordained. Don't wallow in dismay; turn every setback into a catalyst for a more meaningful tomorrow.

The Privilege of Prayer

לְאִישׁ הַיִּשְׂרְאֵלִי הָרְשָׁה לוֹמַר וּלְקַלֵּם בְּכָל עֵת וּזְמַן וּלְהַאֲרִיךְ
בְּכָל מִינֵי קִלּוּסִין וְשִׁירוֹת וְתִשְׁבָּחוֹת... אֲפִילוּ אִם הַמֶּלֶךְ הוּא
בְּכַעַס, כַּאֲשֶׁר רוֹאֶה בְּנוֹ חֲבִיבוֹ נִכְנָס שִׂמְחָה וְתַעֲנוּג לְאָבִיו,
וְהִנֵּה בְּבוֹא הַשִּׂמְחָה וְאַהֲבָה, נִסְתַּלֵּק הַכַּעַס וְהַזַּעַם.

Some angels are only permitted to sing praise before G-d once a week, or even only once every fifty years. When their turn comes, they are exceedingly brief. Some proclaim *kadosh* ("Holy!"), others proclaim *baruch* ("Blessed!"), and still others chant a verse from Psalms, such as *Give thanks to G-d because He is good, for His kindness is eternal!* A Jew, by contrast, may utter praise whenever he wishes and extend all manner of praises and songs.

This can be explained with a parable:

A king ordered his servants and ministers to praise him. Each was allotted a time and duration according to his rank. This continued as long as the king was in a good mood, but if he was furious, they were afraid to praise him at all, as it is stated,

"How can you praise the King at a time of fury!" Due to this concern, they were constantly terrified that something would arouse his displeasure; they offered praise with brevity and left hastily.

The king's son had no such concern. If the king was furious, his anger would melt into joy and delight at the sight of his cherished child. When love and joy arrive in force, they cause fury to rise to its source and become tempered, because severities are sweetened only at their original source.

This is the significance of *Elokim nisah et Avraham*, *G-d tested Abraham*. *Elokim* represents Divine severity. *Nisah*, tested, also means elevate (Exodus 20:17). We can read the verse as follows: *Elokim nisah*, "Divine severity is elevated," *et Avraham*, "with Abraham," through love and kindness, as personified by Abraham, as it is stated, *The loving kindness of Abraham* (Micah 7:20).

FOCUS

You are G-d's cherished child. Pray to Him, thank Him, and connect to Him.

Chayei Sarah

Philanthropy of the Soul

אַבְרָהָם אָבִינוּ עָלָיו הַשָּׁלוֹם הָיָה חָכָם נִפְלָא בְּחָכְמַת הַמֶּחְקָר
הָאֱלֹקִי, וּבְוַדַּאי שֶׁכָּל רֶגַע וָרֶגַע הָיְתָה יְקָרָה לוֹ בְּנַפְשׁוֹ, וְעִם
זֶה הָיָה נָדִיב בְּנַפְשׁוֹ לְהַנִּיחַ אֶת עַצְמוֹ בִּשְׁבִיל לִלְמוֹד עִם
אֲנָשִׁים פְּשׁוּטִים שֶׁאֵינָם מֵעֶרְכּוֹ כְּלָל, כִּי נוֹשֵׂא וְתֹכֶן מַעֲלַת
נָדִיב בְּנַפְשׁוֹ הוּא לְהַנִּיחַ אֶת עַצְמוֹ בִּשְׁבִיל טוֹבַת זוּלָתוֹ.

"There are three kinds of generosity: financial, physical, and intellectual. Our patriarch Abraham excelled in all three."

Indeed, Abraham was generous with his money, his body, and his soul: He used his wealth to provide food and drink to all passersby. He exerted himself physically, personally serving food to those who entered his abode. He sacrificed his soul, his spiritual and intellectual pursuits. For as stated in *Sefer Yetzirah*, Abraham was astoundingly knowledgeable in the fields of theology, and he deeply cherished each moment that he could devote to his own studies and contemplations. Nevertheless, he set aside his soul's spiritual desires for the sake of feeding spirituality to the souls of others, teaching plain folk who were not in his league at all. The defining quality of one who is generous with his soul is to ignore his own spiritual interests for the sake of his fellows.

FOCUS

If you wish to be close to G-d, reach out to others.

The Soul's Pedigree

עֶם אִיז אַ גְרֶעסֶערְע יִחוּס וָאס אִיז מֶער נִיט פַאראַן וָוי בַּא יִצְחָק'ן,
דָאס אִיז "אַבְרָהָם הוֹלִיד אֶת יִצְחָק", וָואס דֶער קְלָסְתֵּר פָּנִים פוּן
אַבְרָהָם הָאט נָאר יִצְחָק, אוּן דָאס אִיבֶּערְגֶעגֶעבְּן צוּ יַעֲקֹב אָבִינוּ
בִּירוּשָׁה לְכָל יִשְׂרָאֵל, אוּן דָאס אִיז "בָּנִים אַתֶּם לַהֲוָי' אֱלֹקיכֶם",
אַז נִשְׁמוֹת יִשְׂרָאֵל זַיְינֶען אַ חֵלֶק מֵעַצְמוּת אֵין סוֹף בָּרוּךְ הוּא.

These are the descendants of Isaac the son of Abraham:
Abraham begot Isaac (Genesis 25:19).

This verse does not contain a redundancy, because it is
insufficient to simply state that Isaac was Abraham's son, as that
would place Isaac on par with Ishmael, who is similarly referred
to as *Ishmael the son of Abraham* (Ibid., v. 12).

True, Isaac's birth was greatly superior, because Ishmael
was born before Abraham received the commandment of
circumcision that brought him the marvelous quality of perfect
faith, whereas Isaac was born after Abraham had become
physically perfect through circumcision. Nevertheless, we could
have erred by assuming that Isaac, like Ishmael, was no more
than a biological son of Abraham.

Therefore, G-d set the record straight: Isaac's pedigree is beyond being *the son of Abraham*. He has the exclusive privilege of *Abraham begot Isaac*. For our Sages explain this phrase to imply that Abraham's facial appearance was replicated only in Isaac. This special pedigree was subsequently transmitted by Isaac exclusively to Jacob, who transmitted it as an eternal inheritance to each subsequent Jew.

You can now appreciate the value of the Jewish souls, as expressed in the verse, *You are sons to the L-rd, your G-d* (Deuteronomy 14:1). You, the Jewish nation, have the exclusive pedigree of being a part of G-d's Infinite Essence.

FOCUS

Never underestimate your worth. You carry G-d within you.

Heaven Is Your Mirror

אָדָם עַל יְדֵי מַעֲשָׂיו הַטּוֹבִים הוּא דָבוּק בּוֹ יִתְבָּרֵךְ מַמָּשׁ, וּכְמוֹ שֶׁכָּתוּב
"וְהָלַכְתָּ בִּדְרָכָיו", וְעַל יְדֵי שֶׁהוּא רַחוּם לְמַטָּה נִתְעוֹרֵר מִדָּה זוֹ שֶׁל
רַחוּם לְמַעֲלָה בְּכָל הָעוֹלָמוֹת, וּכְמוֹ שֶׁכָּתוּב "דַּע מַה לְמַעֲלָה מִמְּךָ",
רוֹצֶה לוֹמַר: מִמְּךָ תֵּדַע אֵיזֶה מִדָּה שֶׁנִּתְעוֹרֵר בְּךָ שֶׁכָּךְ הוּא לְמַעֲלָה.

We must contemplate and remind ourselves that we are *a ladder planted on the ground with its head reaching the heavens* (Genesis 28:12). If we are mindful of the reality that each of our movements, actions, and words generate repercussions in heaven, we will be careful to do everything for the sake of G-d.

Conversely, if we question our ability to damage or repair matters in the heavens and on earth, whereby our every deed has a direct influence Above, we will eventually throw off all responsibility. We will follow our instincts, claiming that there are no consequences.

This is falsehood. Through our good deeds, we literally attach ourselves to G-d Himself, as it is stated, *You shall go in His ways* (Deuteronomy 28:9). Meaning that *His* ways are influenced by the way *we* go: If we act mercifully on earth, the attribute of Divine mercy is awakened in heaven and radiates within all of the worlds. And the same is true of the other attributes.

For it is stated, "Know what is above you..." (Avot 2:1), meaning that the way to "know what is above," i.e., to identify the Divine attribute currently dominating the heavens and influencing its decisions, is from "you," through recognizing the attribute that you are currently projecting.

FOCUS

G-d placed the entire universe in your hands. Fill it with mercy and goodness.

A Message from a Derailed Prayer

"אֱדוֹם" נִקְרָא "הִתְלַהֲבוּת", הָאָדָם שֶׁמִּתְפַּלֵּל בְּהִתְלַהֲבוּת וְשׁוֹלֶטֶת
עָלָיו מַחֲשָׁבָה זָרָה נִקְרָא "בֶּלַע", לְשׁוֹן בְּרִיתָה, "בֶּן", כְּשֶׁהוּא מֵבִין
אֶת זֹאת הַמַּחֲשָׁבָה זָרָה מַה הִיא, "בְּעוֹר", מְבַעֵר אוֹתָהּ.

The *Zohar* states that heaven "judges a person in each chamber and drives him from the chamber." This refers to prayer—each spoken word is a chamber that houses our concentration. As we pray, we move between chambers, from letter to letter and word to word. If our service is deficient, heaven drives us from the chamber, sending us distracting, mundane thoughts. We find ourselves outside, reciting words while concentrating on entirely external thoughts.

The realization that we have been banished shakes us and fills us with determination to improve and concentrate harder. Our derailment thereby propels us to greater enthusiasm, in the spirit of, *Give us assistance from the adversary* (Psalms 60:13)—our assistance is a result of the adversary itself.

This message is encoded in the Torah: *Bela son of Be'or reigned in Edom, and the name of his city was Dinhavah* (Genesis 36:32). Edom means redness, indicating fiery passion, i.e., passionate prayer. Bela implies cutting off. Taken together, Bela's rule over Edom represents our derailed concentration.

Son of Be'or. Ben, son, is related to *bin*, understanding. Be'or means burn. Taken together, it represents our realization that we were banished, along with our reaction—to burn the distracting thoughts by using them as fuel to increase fervor.

Ir, city, is related to the word for arousal. What is "the name of his city," meaning the cause of our arousal to superior prayer? Dinhavah—from the word *din*, judgment. Our realization that heaven passed judgment on our prayers.

> **FOCUS**
>
> Derailment is a wink from Above, telling you that you are capable of more.

The Secret Behind Cravings

❧

לָמָה בָּרָא הַקָּדוֹשׁ בָּרוּךְ הוּא דִּבְרֵי מַאֲכָל וּמַשְׁקֶה שֶׁאָדָם תָּאֵב לָהֶם?
וְהַטַּעַם שֶׁהֵם נִיצוֹץ אָדָם הָרִאשׁוֹן שֶׁהָיוּ מִתְלַבְּשִׁים בְּדוֹמֵם־צוֹמֵחַ־
חַי־מְדַבֵּר וְיֵשׁ לָהֶם חֵשֶׁק לְהִדָּבֵק בִּקְדֻשָּׁה, וְהֵם מְעוֹרְרִים מַיִּין נוּקְבִין
בְּסוֹד אֵין טִפָּה יוֹרְדָה מִלְמַעְלָה שֶׁאֵין טִפַּיִם עוֹלִים כְּנֶגְדָּהּ, וְכָל אֲכִילָה
שֶׁאָדָם אוֹכֵל וְשׁוֹתֶה הִיא מַמָּשׁ חֵלֶק נִיצוֹצוֹת שֶׁלּוֹ שֶׁהוּא צָרִיךְ לְתַקֵּן.

❧

When Judah saw her, he thought she was a harlot, because she covered her face (Genesis 38:15).

The word for face, *panim*, indicates *penimiyus*, internal. Outwardly, she appeared to be seeking material gratification, but her inner intent was to be elevated to sanctity through her soul's attachment to Judah's soul.

This reflects the mystical purpose of our interactions with materiality—food, drink, and so on:

G-d created everything with words, as our Sages state, "The world was created via ten utterances" (Avot 5:1). G-d's words, *yehi raki'a* (*Let there be a firmament!* (Genesis 1:6)), created the heavens and constantly sustains them. The same goes for, *Let the earth produce creatures!* (ibid., v. 24), *Let the earth produce vegetation!* (ibid., v. 11), and so on. These Divine utterances are further stimulated by our own utterances: When we recite a blessing over a fruit with concentration, pronouncing G-d's holy name, the Divine energy that sustains that fruit awakens, and it energizes our own souls.

It is stated, *Hungry and thirsty, their soul enwraps itself in them* (Psalms 107:5). Why did G-d design us with cravings for food and drink? Because the Divine energy within materiality longs to be reattached to sanctity. Food appeals to our corporeal senses to arouse our appetite and thirst, but only so that we can reconnect its soul to sanctity. Physical appeal is a garb, disguising the quest of the sparks to reconnect with G-d. Do not be misled into focusing on the materiality; realize that it is soul calling unto soul.

FOCUS

Behind every craving lies a universe pleading for your spiritual attention.

Comparing Individuals

כִּי לַחְקוֹר מִי נָבוֹן וְחָכָם צָרִיךְ שֶׁיִּהְיֶה זֶה יוֹתֵר נָבוֹן וְחָכָם שֶׁיַּחְקוֹר אוֹתוֹ,
וְזֶה לֹא נִמְצָא יוֹתֵר נָבוֹן וְחָכָם מִיּוֹסֵף שֶׁיַּחְקוֹר אוֹתוֹ, לְכָךְ "אֵין נָבוֹן וְחָכָם".

*Pharaoh told his servants, "Will we find someone like this,
a man in whom there is the spirit of G-d?" Pharaoh then said to
Joseph, "Since G-d has let you know all this, there is no one as
understanding and wise as you!"* (Genesis 41:38-39).

According to our Sages, Pharaoh declared to his officers, "If
we were to go around and seek, would we find anyone like him?"

In other words: We may discover other individuals with
extraordinary intellectual capabilities, but how would we ever
know for certain whether they are like him?

In order to properly evaluate an individual's wisdom and
understanding, a person of superior wisdom is required to
conduct the testing. The Egyptians recognized that no one
in their own ranks of wise men and scholars was greater in

wisdom and understanding than Joseph. It would therefore be impossible—even if they were to discover another extremely wise individual—to compare that other genius with Joseph, because they were incapable of conducting a test to compare Joseph with another candidate.

FOCUS

Before you can judge others, you have to truly understand them.

Approaching a Tzaddik

יֵשׁ ב׳ סוּגִים אֲנָשִׁים, א׳ הַמִּתְנַהֵג עַל פִּי הַטֶּבַע, שֶׁהוּא גִּימַטְרִיָּא אֱלֹקִים,
הַנִּקְרָא יְהוּדָה מַלְכוּת, ב׳ הַמִּתְנַהֵג לְמַעֲלָה מֵהַטֶּבַע, בְּחִינַת צַדִּיק מוֹשֵׁל
בְּיִרְאַת אֱלֹקִים שֶׁהוּא מְבַטֵּל גְּזֵרַת אֱלֹקִים, וְזֶה נִקְרָא "יוֹסֵף הַצַּדִּיק".
וְכַאֲשֶׁר אֶחָד בְּאֶחָד יִגַּשׁוּ וְנִתְחַבְּרוּ ב׳ סוּגִים הַנַּ״ל נַעֲשֶׂה הַכֹּל בְּחִינָה אַחַת.

Then Judah approached him [Joseph]... (Genesis 44:18).

Our nation is comprised of two kinds of souls: the ordinary
Jew and the *tzaddik* (righteous person).

An ordinary Jew conducts himself according to the laws of
nature. The numerical value of *hateva*, nature, is 86, which is the
same value as the Divine name Elokim, the force that sustains
and operates within all of nature. Elokim is also referred to
as "Judah," because Judah embodied the Divine attribute of
malchut (royalty), and Elokim is associated with *malchut*, the
attribute through which everything was created.

The *tzaddik*, by contrast, operates in a supernatural manner and is described as *the righteous who rule through their awe of G-d* (II Samuel 23:3). They rule over nature because they hold sway over the Divine name Elokim, overriding heavenly decrees that come into effect through that level of Divinity. A *tzaddik* is referred to as Yosef HaTzaddik (Joseph the Righteous).

The Torah describes Judah approaching and drawing close to Joseph. This alludes to an ordinary Jew approaching a *tzaddik*, whereby the two kinds of Jewish souls are united. The ordinary Jew becomes a throne for the *tzaddik*, meaning that the *tzaddik* is able to work supernaturally through the agency of the Jew who operates according to the laws of nature.

FOCUS

Follow the directives of the Rebbe and watch the natural course take supernatural twists.

Experience Breeds Sensitivity

וְזֶהוּ שֶׁכָּתוּב "וַיְחִי יַעֲקֹב בְּאֶרֶץ מִצְרַיִם", רוֹצֶה לוֹמַר: עַל יְדֵי הַגָּלוּת
וְהַצָּרוֹת וְהַמֵּיצָרִים שֶׁהָיָה לְיַעֲקֹב, יָדַע לְהִתְפַּלֵּל מִזֶּה עַל חֶסְרוֹן
הַשְּׁכִינָה, שֶׁנִּקְרָא גַּם כֵּן יַעֲקֹב, וְשַׁפִּיר קָאָמַר "וַיְחִי יַעֲקֹב", שֶׁחִבֵּר
הַשְּׁכִינָה אֶל חַי הַחַיִּים עַל יְדֵי הַמְּצֵרִים, וּבַצָּר הִרְחַבְתָּ לִי.

Jacob lived in the land of Egypt for seventeen years (Genesis 47:28).

The mystical meaning of this verse is similar to that of, *In my distress You have relieved [hirchavta] me"* (Psalms 4:2): The distress itself is the cause of the expansiveness (*harchavah*)—the abundance of blessings that follow.

Tzaddikim are emissaries of the *Shechinah* (Divine Presence). Their role is to pray for the welfare of the *Shechinah*, which languishes in exile. When a *tzaddik* suffers from lack or from exile, he arrives at a fuller appreciation for the plight of the *Shechinah*. He is then in a better position to pray for the *Shechinah*.

This is alluded to in the Torah's description of the years that our patriarch Jacob spent in Egypt: *Jacob lived in the land of Egypt…* The Hebrew name for Egypt, *Mitzrayim*, is related to *meitzarim*, distress and constraints. Through the exile and constraints that Jacob personally experienced, he understood how to pray for the equivalent experiences of the *Shechinah*.

This verse also alludes to the success of Jacob's subsequent prayers. For the *Shechinah* is also referred to as "Jacob." In that case, the phrase *Jacob lived* indicates that through his prayers, our patriarch Jacob caused the *Shechinah* ("Jacob") to live—to unite with the supernal source of life. And all this occurred *in the land of Egypt*—as a result of his being forced to personally experience suffering.

FOCUS

Negative experiences prepare us to better assist others in suffering.

Liberating the World

עוֹלָם הַזֶּה וֶוערט אָנגערופֿן צָרָה וֶוייל עֶר אִיז אַ מָקוֹם צָר. דִי
עוֹלָמוֹת הָעֶלְיוֹנִים וֶואוּ דֶער אוֹר אֵין סוֹף אִיז בְּגִילוּי זַיִינֶען אַ
מָקוֹם רָחָב, אָבֶּער דֶער עוֹלָם הַזֶּה וֶואוּ דֶער אוֹר אֵין סוֹף אִיז
מְלוּבָּשׁ בְּדַרְכֵי הַטֶּבַע, אִיז דָאס אַ מָקוֹם צָר אוּן דֶערוּם וֶוערט
עוֹלָם הַזֶּה אָנגערופֿן צָרָה. דִי כַּוָוּנָה הָעֶלְיוֹנָה אִיז אַז דוּרְךְ דֶער
עֲבוֹדָה אִין לִמּוּד הַתּוֹרָה אוּן קִיּוּם הַמִּצְוֹת זָאל מֶען מַאכן פֿוּן
צָרָה צָהַר, בַּאלייכטן דִי וֶועלט מִיט דֶעם אוֹר הַתּוֹרָה וּמִצְוֹת.

*An angel of G-d appeared to him in a flame of fire from within
the thorn bush* (Exodus 3:2).

Why did G-d's emissary appear within a prickly plant?
Rashi clarifies: "Specifically a thorn bush, and not another kind
of shrub, in order to convey the message that *I am with you in
distress* (Psalms 91:14)."

In its broadest meaning, the term *tzarah*, "distress," includes
the entire physical existence. It is referred to as *tzarah* because it
is a dimension of extreme constraint (*tzar*).

The upper realms of existence are spiritual, and they are unconstrained by comparison, basking in the overt revelation of G-d's Infinite Light. They and their contents are therefore expansive.

In this world, however, the Infinite Light expresses itself through the dense veil of nature. The result is a dimension of extreme spiritual constraint and concealment. As a consequence, our physical world becomes a place of *tzarah*, distress.

But it was not meant to remain that way:

G-d's intention in creating the world in such a manner was to give room for our input. Through our Divine service of Torah study and observing the *mitzvot*, we transform the *tzarah* (צרה), "distress," into *tzohar* (צהר), "luminance." We illuminate the universe with the light of Torah and *mitzvot*, so that Divine revelation can replace the concealment.

FOCUS

Your study and good deeds are powerful tools of transformation.

The Dishonor of
Chasing Honor

וְצָרִיךְ לָזֶה הָאֱמָנָה לִתְלוֹת הַחִסָּרוֹן תָּמִיד בּוֹ, וְלַחֲפּוֹץ תָּמִיד בִּכְנִיעָה
וְשִׁפְלוּת אֲפִילוּ לִדְבַר מִצְוָה, פֶּן וְאוּלַי הוּא מִצַּד הַגַּבְהוּת שֶׁל
הַקְּלִפָּה לַעֲשׂוֹת מִצְוָה שֶׁאֵינָה מֻטֶּלֶת עָלָיו, וְשֶׁיּוּכַל לַעֲשׂוֹת עַל יְדֵי
אַחֵר, וְלֹא יַחְשׁוֹב שֶׁהוּא רָאוּי לָהּ יוֹתֵר מֵחֲבֵרוֹ, כִּי זֶהוּ גַבְהוּת.

The Torah testifies that Moses was exceedingly humble, but
even Moses exercised his authority as necessary. He was the
king of the Jews and conducted himself accordingly, but solely in
the service of G-d—to train the nation to serve G-d.

Moses did not want to rule. He refused the position:
*I beseech You, G-d, send now using the agency of the one [i.e.,
Aaron] whom You would [regularly] send* (4:13), but G-d forced
leadership upon him.

When Korah challenged that leadership, Moses responded,
Rav lachem bnei Levi—It is enough for you, sons of Levi! (Numbers
16:7). Meaning, your self-promotion is not for G-d's sake, but

rav lachem—the *rav,* "greatness," you demand, is *lachem,* "for yourselves."

It is difficult to avoid shedding our humility while pursuing a mitzvah. We are focused on our spiritual opportunity, but wait—perhaps this mitzvah does not belong to us; perhaps someone else is more fitting for it. To grab it for ourselves is highly arrogant. Is there a greater mitzvah than to lead and teach Torah to the entire nation? And yet Moses declined the opportunity because he felt that Aaron was a better candidate.

Do not quarrel over the right to perform a mitzvah involving any form of authority or control. Flee from such arguments! If it is for you, G-d will compel the entire world to place it in your hands without you having to compete or promote yourself. Pray that G-d assists you in avoiding this trap.

FOCUS

Humility is always important. If you need to be in a position of authority, G-d will find His way to put you there. Don't let it be the source of a quarrel.

A Midnight Moment

"וַיְהִי כַּחֲצוֹת הַלַּיְלָה", שֶׁהַסָּפֵק הוּא "כַּחֲצוֹת" לְכַאן וּלְכַאן, אָז
"אֲנִי" ה' "יוֹצֵא בְּתוֹךְ מִצְרָיִם", בַּמֵּצַר שֶׁלּוֹ, לְהָאִיר עֵינָיו.

The spirit of G-d was hovering over the face of the water. And G-d said: Let there be light (Genesis 1:2-3).

What is the spirit of G-d? It is the soul within you. It hovers over the surface of your water, meaning the Torah that you study, because the Torah is compared to water. You hover with all your soul over a single topic, unable to continue your journey through the ocean of Torah wisdom, because you cannot reach a true conclusion in a topic with which you are experiencing difficulty. You hover because you care too deeply to move on.

G-d then announces, *Let there be light!* He commands that your eyes be illuminated by the light of Torah, so that you can resolve the matter with sudden clarity.

At around the dividing point of the night (midnight), *I will go out into the midst of Egypt* (11:4). The word *kachatzos*, *at around midnight*, indicates a doubt whether that precise moment belongs to the first or second half of the night. *Kachatzos* alludes to a Torah concept that lacks clarity.

Due to your diligence in toiling over the issue, G-d announces, *I will go out into the midst of Egypt*. G-d intervenes to rescue you from your intellectual constraint—*Mitzrayim* (Egypt) is related to *meitzarim* (constraint). He will illuminate your eyes with the Torah's truth.

FOCUS

If you care and you try, you will succeed beyond your current abilities.

When Fleeing Is Useless

מִי שֶׁרוֹצָה לִפְטוֹר מֵהַצַּר וְהַמֵּצָר וְהוּא נוֹסֵעַ אַחֲרָיו, מָשָׁל לְאִשָּׁה
יוֹלֶדֶת שֶׁהָלְכָה לְמָקוֹם אַחֵר לִפְטוֹר מֵחֶבְלֵי הַלֵּדָה וְהַצַּעַר הוֹלֵךְ
אַחֲרֶיהָ. וְעֵצָה הַיְעוּצָה שֶׁיִּתְפַּלֵּל לְהַשֵּׁם יִתְבָּרֵךְ וְיִפְּטֵר מֵהַצַּעַר.
וְזֶהוּ שֶׁכָּתוּב "מִן הַמֵּצַר קָרָאתִי יָּהּ עָנָנִי בַמֶּרְחָב יָהּ".

The children of Israel lifted up their eyes and behold, the Egyptians were advancing after them. They were very frightened, and the children of Israel cried out to G-d (Exodus 14:10).

Leaving Egypt was insufficient, because Egypt came out with them. To what is this comparable? To one who relocates in order to flee internal pain or distress, only to discover that wherever he goes, his internal condition accompanies him. It is like a woman hoping to quiet her labor pains by hurrying to a different location, only to realize that the pain is still with her.

Rather, our only solution is to cry out to G-d and ask Him to remove the cause of our suffering, as it is stated, *From the straits* [meitzar] *I called G-d; G-d answered me with a vast expanse* (Psalms 118:5).

This is the deeper significance of the verse, *The Egyptians were advancing after them. Mitzrayim*, Egypt, is related to *meitzarim*, troubles and distress, which like the Egyptains, tend to follow a person who attempts only a physical escape.

Recognizing this truth, *The children of Israel cried out to G-d*, praying for a permanent solution. They were subsequently informed, *As you have seen the Egyptians today, you shall no longer continue to see them for eternity* (ibid., v. 13), meaning, the troubles that you experience at present will be permanently solved.

FOCUS

Recognize that G-d is the cause of all events; go straight to the Top.

YITRO

Burned Out

לְכָךְ כָּפָה הַקָּדוֹשׁ בָּרוּךְ הוּא עַל יִשְׂרָאֵל הַר כְּגִיגִית, לְלַמֵּד שֶׁגַּם שֶׁאֵינוֹ חוֹשֵׁק לְתוֹרָה וַעֲבוֹדַת ה', מִכָּל מָקוֹם אֵינוֹ בֶּן חוֹרִין לִבָּטֵל, רַק יַעֲשֶׂה בְּעַל כָּרְחוֹ וִידַמֶּה כְּמִי שֶׁכּוֹפִּוֹ אוֹתוֹ לַעֲשׂוֹתוֹ בְּעַל כָּרְחוֹ.

As our ancestors prepared to receive the Torah at Sinai, *they stood at the bottom of the mountain* (Exodus 19:17). Not at the foot of the mountain, but at its bottom, i.e., underneath the actual mountain, for our Sages taught in the name of R. Avdimi ben Chama ben Chasa: "This verse informs us that the Holy One, Blessed be He, held the mountain over them like a barrel."

Was it necessary for G-d to threaten the Jews by suspending a mountain over their heads? Did they not willingly declare, *naaseh v'nishma—we will do and we will obey* (Exodus 24:7)?

Rather, this addresses a common obstacle in Torah study: We may be inspired to study Torah and dive into its Divine wisdom with enthusiasm. After some time, we suddenly find our passion waning until we are left spiritually dry. At that point, it is hard to continue, and we are wracked with disappointment over our inability to experience our former enthusiasm for G-d's holy Torah.

The solution is to replicate the Giving of the Torah at Sinai: The Jews arrived with tremendous enthusiasm, but then G-d held a mountain over their heads to impart the message: When your passion fades, apply yourself to your studies as if compelled, as if a mountain were suspended over your heads, for even the words of Torah you utter without enthusiasm remain sacred.

FOCUS

Do what is right, regardless of your feelings.

Negligence in
Divine Service

"עַל שׁוֹר" — שׁוֹר אִיז דֶער יֵצֶר הָרָע... "עַל חֲמוֹר" — חֲמוֹר
אִיז קְרִירוּת... "עַל שֶׂה" — שֶׂה פְּזוּרָה, עֶר צוּשְׁפְּרֵייט זִיךְ
אִין אַלֶעם, אַלֶעם וְויל עֶר, אַלֶעם דַאְרף עֶר, "עַל שַׂלְמָה" —
שַׂלְמָה מֵיינְט דִי לְבוּשִׁים, "עַל כָּל אֲבֵדָה" — וָואס דוּרְךְ דֶעם
פַאְרְלִירְט עֶר אַלֶעם אוּן וֵוייסְט נִיט בַּיי וָואס עֶר הַאלְט.

*For any matter of negligence: for an ox, donkey, lamb, garment;
for any lost object...* (Exodus 22:8).

A guardian employed to protect someone's asset is
financially responsible for negligence. *Pesha*, negligence, is the
acronym of *perikut shel ol*, casting off [Heaven's] yoke. The phrase
For any matter of negligence implies that the cause of all spiritual
ills is a deficit in our subservience to G-d's will.

But how can a Jew reject G-d's will? Is a Jew not holy, born
in purity through the use of a kosher *mikveh*, which contains
purifying power that is a *chok*, a Divine decree that transcends

logic? Such laws are intrinsically associated with subservience to G-d's will!? Furthermore, the angels warm themselves by water heated for a *mikveh*, and accompany the soul as it descends into a body. So how then can a Jew reject G-d's will?

The answer: *An ox*, our *yetzer hara* (evil inclination), whose source is the celestial *"face of an ox"* [as described by the prophet (Ezekiel 1:10)]. *A donkey*, spiritual frigidity, as the Talmud states, "A donkey feels chilly even in midsummer's heat"; similarly, our *yetzer hara* cools off our passion for G-d's service—*G-d is a sun* (Psalms 84:12).

A sheep, distraction, as in, *a scattered sheep* (Jeremiah 50:17); we are unfocused, scattering our attention in all directions, wanting everything. *A garment*, our soul's soiled garments of inappropriate thought, speech, and deed. *For any lost object*, we lose recognition of our dismal spiritual status. There is only one way to avoid these pitfalls: *kabbalat ol*—accepting the yoke of heaven unconditionally.

FOCUS

Do everything for G-d's sake, not for yours; you can't go wrong.

Sources of Inspiration

'מִשֶּׁחָרַב בֵּית הַמִּקְדָּשׁ אֵין לוֹ לְהַקָּדוֹשׁ בָּרוּךְ הוּא בְּעוֹלָמוֹ אֶלָּא ד'
אַמּוֹת שֶׁל הֲלָכָה' — די ד' אַמּוֹת וואָס מאַכן אים פּאַר אַ מְהַלֵּךְ

Our Sages declared: Ever since the Holy Temple was destroyed, all that G-d has in His world is the four cubits of *halachah.*

Their wording is precise. They did not state that G-d is found in the teachings of *halachah* or in its application. Rather, they emphasized the *daled amot* (four cubits) of *halachah*, meaning the physical space within which *halachah* is found. This is to be understood as follows:

The term for Jewish law, *halachah*, derives from the verb *halach*, to go, to proceed. G-d is present—to a degree similar to His presence in the Holy Temple—within the setting that inspires a person to become a *mehaleich*, to proceed and advance in Divine service. In other words, during exile, any setting, event, or gathering that inspires us to advance spiritually is where G-d's presence is to be found.

The Arizal taught that the term for Jewish law, *HaLaCHaH*, is an acronym for *Hari'u Lashem Kol Ha'aretz—Shout joyfully to G-d, all the earth!* (Psalms 100:1).

The word *halachah* is derived from *halichah*, proceeding. How do we proceed in our Divine service? Through *hari'u* (shout joyfully), which also means to shatter, as in the verse, *You will shatter them [tero'eim] with an iron rod* (Psalms 2:9). We must break "*the earth*," our coarse corporeality and unrefined traits.

When a student is tested on *halachah*, the examiner attempts to mislead him with difficult questions. Similarly, G-d tests our *halichah*, our progress in Divine service, with a *yetzer hara* that employs confusion and raises questions. If we are wise, we will not fall for its tricks.

G-d will then delight in our conduct, just as a parent delights in his child who refuses to be defeated by misleading questions and passes his test with wisdom.

FOCUS

Cherish inspirational people and events—G-d certainly does.

Yehei Shemei Rabba

הֲגַם עָם זַיינֶען דָא דַרְגוֹת, "יִשְׁכּוֹן חֲצֵרֶיךָ בֵּיתֶךָ קְדוֹשׁ הֵיכָלֶךָ
וגו'", מִכָּל מָקוֹם אִיז בַּיי אָמֵן יְהֵא שְׁמֵי' רַבָּא זַיינֶען אַלֶע גְלַייךָ.

Praiseworthy is he whom You choose and draw near to dwell in Your courts; let us be sated with the goodness of Your house, the sanctity of Your Temple (Psalms 65:5).

Ashrei, "praiseworthy," is an acronym for the phrase of praise we recite in response to *kaddish: Amein Yehei SHemei Rabba.* The continuation of the above verse describes various levels of spiritual attainment—there are those who are able to *dwell in Your courts*, and others who are able to bask in *the sanctity of*

Your Temple. Nevertheless, the first of all praises, the sanctity associated with *ashrei*, the heartfelt recital of *amein yehei shemei rabba*, is equally available to each Jew.

Tricking the Trickster

וְזֶהוּ שֶׁכָּתוּב 'יִשְׂרָאֵל גַּנָּבִים הֵם', כִּי צָרִיךְ לִגְנוֹב דַּעַת הַיֵּצֶר
הָרָע בְּכָל דְּבַר מִצְוָה. וְזֶהוּ שֶׁכָּתוּב "חִשַּׁבְתִּי דְרָכָי", רוֹצֶה לוֹמַר:
בְּכָל דְּבַר מִצְוָה אוֹ קְדֻשָּׁה בְּהַתְחָלָה חִשַּׁבְתִּי דְרָכַי לַהֲנָאָתִי
הַגַּשְׁמִי, וְאַחַר כָּךְ "וָאָשִׁיבָה רַגְלַי אֶל עֵדוֹתֶיךָ", רוֹצֶה לוֹמַר:
רַגְלֵי הַהֶרְגֵּל שֶׁהָרְגַּל אֶצְלִי שֶׁלֹּא לִשְׁמָהּ, אָז עָשִׂיתִי לִשְׁמָהּ.

I considered my ways, and I returned my feet to Your testimonies (Psalms 119:59).

It is stated, *There is no righteous man on earth who does good and does not sin* (Ecclesiastes 7:20). It is impossible to do only good without initially including a motivation that is non-altruistic or relatively sinful, however slight, because the *yetzer hara* grows extremely agitated at purely good deeds, and it will use its full power to interfere.

By contrast, if it recognizes an element of itself in your motivation, it will leave you alone, at which point you may complete your activity with absolutely pure intentions.

The Midrash tells us that Satan, the prosecuting angel, raises criticism against us, claiming that "Jews are thieves". The true meaning of this is, that indeed we must. steal the mind of our *yetzer hara*, fooling it into trusting that we are not entirely altruistic, so as to avoid its harassment.

This is the deeper significance of the above verse: *I considered my ways*. I deliberately considered my personal benefit from an activity that involves a mitzvah or act of sanctity. Then, *I returned my feet to Your testimonies*. The word *regel*, foot, is associated with *regilut*, regularity and habitual practice. In other words, after an initial thought of personal benefit, which is instinctive, I will return my focus to performing the mitzvah entirely for the right reasons, without any personal interest at all.

FOCUS Self-serving motivations can be turned into perfect springboards for altruism.

Slaughterer in Disguise

'קָדְשֵׁי קָדָשִׁים שְׁחִיטָתָן בַּצָּפוֹן' וְ'קָדָשִׁים קַלִּים בְּכָל
מָקוֹם', שֶׁהַיֵּצֶר הָרָע בָּא אֶל הַתַּלְמִידֵי חֲכָמִים בִּדְמוּת יֵצֶר
הַטּוֹב לַעֲשׂוֹת מִצְוָה, מַה שֶּׁאֵין כֵּן לַהֲמוֹנֵי עָם.

The Mishnah demarcates areas for ritual slaughter within the *azarah*, the Temple Courtyard adjacent to the altar. It states that *kodshei kadashim*, offerings of greater sanctity, may only be slaughtered *batzafon*, in the north, whereas *kadashim kalim*, offerings of lesser sanctity, may be slaughtered at any place [within the courtyard].

There is a deeper message: The *yetzer hara* engages in spiritual slaughter by tricking a person into sinning. He has two kinds of victims. The first is *kodshei kadashim*, those who sincerely devote their lives to Torah study and Divine service. They can only be slaughtered (led to sin) *batzafon*, in the north, meaning, *batzafun*, through a disguise. The *yetzer hara* must disguise itself as a *yetzer tov*, advocating an action that is ostensibly positive but is not what it seems.

Its other victims are *kadashim kalim*, ordinary people, who are spiritually slaughtered in any place, north or otherwise. For them, the *yetzer hara* does not always need a disguise.

FOCUS

Cross check every action by considering its practical consequence.

PEKUDEI

Sidetracked by Glitter

הַשֵּׁם יִתְבָּרֵךְ מְלֹא כָל הָאָרֶץ כְּבוֹדוֹ וְכָל תְּנוּעָה וּמַחֲשָׁבָה הַכֹּל מִמֶּנּוּ
יִתְבָּרֵךְ, [אִם] כֵּן כָּל הַמַּלְאָכִים [וְכָל] הַהֵיכָלוֹת הַכֹּל נִבְרָא וְנַעֲשָׂה
כִּבְיָכוֹל מֵעַצְמוּתוֹ יִתְבָּרֵךְ 'כְּהָדֵין קַמְצָא דִלְבוּשֵׁיה מִנֵּיה וּבֵיה',
וְאֵין שׁוּם מְחִיצָה מַבְדִּיל בֵּין הָאָדָם וּבֵינוֹ יִתְבָּרֵךְ בִּידִיעָה זֹאת.

There is no place void of G-d, as it is stated, *The entire universe is filled with His glory* (Isaiah 6:3). In that case, why are there myriads of angels waiting to raise our prayers through myriads of heavenly chambers? Surely, G-d is present everywhere and can receive our prayers directly?

There was once a wise king who constructed an illusion of multiple gateways and formidable towers. He ordered that whoever wished to approach him had to first proceed through this daunting course. He instructed that treasures be scattered at the various gateways. As a result, people seeking an audience with the king reached one or a few of these entrances before becoming sidetracked by dazzling treasures and returning with riches but without meeting the king. Only the king's own beloved son fortified himself to ignore the towers and treasures, so strong was his desire to see his father, the king. He then realized that no barrier could separate him from the king, because it was all superficial.

G-d hides behind multiple screens and barriers, but in truth, He fills all of existence, and every movement and thought comes from Him. The countless angels and heavenly chambers are created by Him, similar to the concept of a snail that generates its own shell—so that what appears to be a hard covering is actually an integral part of itself. It is all for the sake of making G-d appear distant so that we fortify ourselves to draw closer to G-d with all our strength. Armed with this awareness, nothing can separate us from G-d, and we can dispel the forces of evil, because they are only superficial.

FOCUS

G-d is closer than you think; keep your focus.

Useful Pride

הָרֶמֶז בִּשְׂאוֹר וּדְבַשׁ לְגַבְהוּת שֶׁהֵם מַרְתִּיחִים וְעוֹלִים כְּמוֹ הַגַּבְהוּת
שֶׁמַּגְבִּיהַּ לֵב הָאָדָם... וְאָמַר הַכָּתוּב "לֹא תַקְטִירוּ מִמֶּנּוּ אִשֶּׁה לַה'"
לַעֲבוֹד עַל יְדֵי גַבְהוּת, רַק קָרְבַּן רֵאשִׁית, רוֹצֶה לוֹמַר: רֵאשִׁית הַהִתְקָרְבוּת
לְהַשֵּׁם יִתְבָּרֵךְ מֻתָּר לִהְיוֹת בְּגַבְהוּת, אֲבָל אַחַר כָּךְ "אֶל הַמִּזְבֵּחַ"
הָעֶלְיוֹן "לֹא יַעֲלוּ לְרֵיחַ נִיחוֹחַ לַה'", שֶׁאֵין נַחַת רוּחַ לְפָנָיו יִתְבָּרֵךְ
בְּגַבְהוּת חַס וְשָׁלוֹם, כִּי "תּוֹעֲבַת ה' כָּל גְּבַהּ לֵב", אֲפִילוּ בְּכָל דְּהוּ.

Do not cause to go up in smoke any leavening or honey as a fire offering to G-d; bring them as a first-offering to G-d, but they should not go up on the altar as a pleasing fragrance to G-d (Leviticus 2:11-12).

Leavening and honey are agents that cause dough to ferment and rise. They therefore represent self-importance—a heart swollen with pride and arrogance. Such substances cannot become a fire-offering to G-d, meaning that our Divine service cannot be conducted in such a spirit.

There is an exception: *Bring them as a first-offering to G-d.* A first-offering represents the outset of our Divine service, at which point it is permissible to approach G-d out of a sense of self-worth. In other words, if a lack of pride would prevent you from engaging in Divine service due to your feeling inferior or unworthy, or if you imagine that your input has no effect in heaven, then your first steps ("first-offering") may indeed be conducted with pride.

Nevertheless, once you are well engaged in Divine service and the above concerns dissipate, *they should not go up on the altar as a pleasing fragrance to G-d*—He will not find your self-importance pleasing at all, because even a trace of arrogance is an abomination.

FOCUS

Pat yourself on the back, but know when to stop.

Tzav

Sacrifice in Spirit

כָּל הָעוֹסֵק בְּתוֹרַת עוֹלָה כְּאִלּוּ הִקְרִיב עוֹלָה׳, מִפְּנֵי שֶׁכַּאֲשֶׁר
הוּא מְדַבֵּר בְּאוֹתָן הַדִּבּוּרִים בְּיִרְאָה וּבְאַהֲבָה אָז הוּא נוֹתֵן חַיּוּת
חָדָשׁ בְּאֵלּוּ הַדִּבּוּרִים. אֲבָל כְּשֶׁהָיָה בֵּית הַמִּקְדָּשׁ קַיָּם וְהָיָה
מַקְרִיב קָרְבַּן עוֹלָה הָיָה נוֹתֵן כֹּחַ אַף בְּעוֹלָם הַמַּעֲשֶׂה.

Our Sages state that "whoever occupies himself with the study of *olah* [the laws of the burnt-offering] is considered as having offered an actual *olah*."

How can mere study equal an actual event?

When we read the words of Torah regarding the *olah* with passionate feelings of love and awe of G-d, we breathe new spiritual vitality into the Torah's words. This does not remain as mere spoken words, because in the spiritual realms, the vitality caused by our emotions produces an effect equivalent to an actual offering in the Holy Temple. In the spiritual realms, we have indeed offered an *olah*.

All the same, such an achievement does not replace a tangible offering, because a physical sacrifice introduces new spiritual vitality even to this physical world of action.

> **FOCUS**
>
> Thought, speech, and emotion are extremely powerful, but action trumps them all.

Restoring a Diamond

וְהַמָּשָׁל לְמֶלֶךְ שֶׁנֶּאֶבְדָה לוֹ אֶבֶן טוֹב מִתּוֹךְ טַבַּעְתּוֹ... צִוָּה לִבְנוֹ יְחִידוֹ
וַחֲבִיבוֹ שֶׁיְחַפֵּשׁ וְיִמְצָא הָאֲבֵדָה... רָמַז לִבְנוֹ חֲבִיבוֹ בְּכַמָּה רְמָזִים מְקוֹם
מְצִיאוּתוֹ, כִּי מִתְּחִלָּה הָיְתָה הָאֲבֵדָה מִדַּעַת הַמֶּלֶךְ אֶת מְקוֹמָהּ וְעָשָׂה הַכֹּל
רַק לְמַעַן לְזַכּוֹת אֶת בְּנוֹ חֲבִיבוֹ, וּכְדֵי שֶׁיַּגִּיעַ גַּם לְהַמֶּלֶךְ מִזֶּה גֹּדֶל שֶׁעֲשׁוּעַ
וְהִתְפָּאֲרוּת מִבְּנוֹ לֵאמֹר רְאוּ כִּי שׁוּם בֶּן אָדָם בָּעוֹלָם לֹא הָיָה יָכוֹל לַחְפּוֹשׁ
וְלִמְצוֹא זוּלַת בְּנוֹ חֲבִיבוֹ. וְהַנִּמְשָׁל מוּבָן, שֶׁתְּחִלַּת בְּרִיאַת הָעוֹלָמוֹת הָיָה
כְּדֵי לְבָרֵר הַנִּיצוֹצִין קַדִּישִׁין עַל יְדֵי אֻמָּה יִשְׂרָאֵלִית, כְּמוֹ שֶׁכָּתוּב 'בִּשְׁבִיל
יִשְׂרָאֵל שֶׁנִּקְרָא רֵאשִׁית', שֶׁעַל יָדָם יְבָרְרוּ מִמַּאֲכָלִים מֻתָּרִים וּכְשֵׁרִים.

A king lost a precious diamond that had been set in his ring. Despite having scores of servants, officers, nobles, dukes, and military personnel at his service, he did not command them to search for his gem.

Instead, he commanded his only son to conduct the search. The king knew that his officers were highly capable and guaranteed to succeed, but he wished to credit his precious son with the jewel's recovery.

The king aided his son by dropping hints, because the gem was not truly lost. It had been planted to justify a search, so as to bring merit to his son. The king longed to delight in his son's success, take pride in his accomplishment, and exclaim, "See! No one was able to find it except for my son!"

This parable allows us to recognize that G-d deliberately created a universe with sparks of holiness trapped within materiality, so that He could instruct His son, the Jewish people, to find them and restore them to Him. In particular, they achieve this through eating food that is kosher.

You might feel drawn to food and drink out of hunger and thirst, but in truth, it is your soul that is attracted to the sparks of holiness trapped within food and drink, because you have received a mission of redeeming these particular sparks. G-d gave us a clear set of instructions as to how we must use and interact with materiality. These are hints, pointing to the sparks that form the basis of our mission. He did not offer these instructions to the countless angels; rather, He lovingly planted the sparks on earth, especially for us.

FOCUS

Treat the Torah's directives as acts of Divine love.

Heartfelt Inspiration

אָדָם עַצְמוֹ עוֹשֶׂה תַּחְבּוּלוֹת לְהִתְעוֹרֵר בִּתְפִלָּה נִקְרָא זָכָר, מַיִּין
דּוּכְרִין, מַה שֶׁאֵין כֵּן שֶׁיֵּשׁ לִפְעָמִים שֶׁמְּעוֹרְרִין אוֹתוֹ מִלְמַעְלָה
[שֶׁמֵּעַצְמוֹ נִתְעוֹרֵר] בִּבְכִיָּה [וְכַיּוֹצֵא] זֶהוּ נִקְרָא אִשָּׁה, מַיִּין נוּקְבִין.

In spiritual terms, when you toil to concentrate and arouse your emotions appropriately during prayer, you experience a masculine effort, actively providing input required for proper prayer. If, instead, you find yourself spontaneously inspired or moved to tears, you experience a feminine effort, passively receiving emotion sent from Above.

Ideally, prayer should be active, not passive. Spontaneous inspiration indicates that heaven is displeased with your lack of adequate effort. You experience an awakening because severities are arrayed against you in heaven, and the root of your soul sees these judgments and fears them. Its terrified reaction filters down to you in this world, appearing in the form of sudden, unearned arousal to serve G-d properly.

To rectify the situation, you must feel remorse over your failure to motivate yourself appropriately, to the point that you had to be jostled from Above. Weep sincerely for any spontaneous tears granted from Above. Then, your experience will be retroactively transformed and regarded in heaven as your very own input.

FOCUS

Cherish your own toil.

Outreach via In-Reach

'אֵיזֶהוּ חָכָם הַלּוֹמֵד מִכָּל אָדָם?', אֲפִילוּ מֵאָדָם רַע שֶׁרוֹאֶה דָבָר
עֲבֵרָה בּוֹ וְלוֹמֵד מִמֶּנּוּ, שֶׁמִּצַּד אַחְדוּת יֵשׁ בּוֹ שֶׁמֶץ מֶנְהוּ גַם כֵּן וְצָרִיךְ
לְתַקֵּן עַצְמוֹ מִשֶּׁמֶץ זֶה שֶׁבּוֹ, וְאָז גּוֹרֵם טָהֳרָה לְזוּלָתוֹ כו', וְזֶהוּ שֶׁכָּתוּב
"זֹאת תּוֹרַת" הַמּוֹצִיא רָע מֵרֵעָתוֹ "בְּיוֹם טָהֳרָתוֹ" שֶׁל עַצְמוֹ.

This is the law of the metzora on the day of his purity (Leviticus 14:2).

All Jews are truly one. Therefore, our Sages state, "Who is wise? He who learns from each person." We can even learn from a wicked individual whom we observe acting in sin. What can we possibly learn from such an encounter?

Seeing that all Jews are truly one entity, we must realize that we harbor a degree of the same sinfulness we observed in our fellow Jew, albeit in an infinitely more subtle form. We must then strive to correct the subtle flaw within ourselves, and as a result of Jewish unity, our positive effort will cause our fellow Jew to become purified and break free from his wickedness.

This is the deeper meaning of the Torah's introduction to the laws of the *metzora*. The term *metzora* can be read as *motzi ra*, "he who extracts evil" from his fellow Jew. When is one able to accomplish this? *On the day of* his *purity*, referring to the day that the person who observed the evil purifies *himself*. Purging himself of subtle wrongs causes his fellow's more intense evil to be extracted and removed.

FOCUS

Experience firsthand the improvement you wish to see in others.

Heaven and Beyond

שֶׁעָקָּר עֵסֶק תּוֹרָה [וּתְפִלָּה] הוּא שֶׁיְּדַבֵּק אֶת עַצְמוֹ אֶל
פְּנִימִיּוּת רוּחָנִיּוּת אוֹר אֵין סוֹף שֶׁבְּתוֹךְ אוֹתִיּוֹת הַתּוֹרָה
[וְהַתְּפִלָּה], שֶׁהוּא הַנִּקְרָא לִמּוּד לִשְׁמָהּ.

Our Sages state, "Four individuals entered the Orchard (*pardeis*)..." Rashi explains that "they ascended Above through the use of the Divine name." *Tosafot* clarifies that "they did not physically ascend, but it seemed to them as if they were in the heavens."

The term *pardeis* (פרדס) is used as a reference to the Torah, because it the acronym for the four rungs of Torah insight: *peshat*, literal interpretation; *remez*, allusion; *derush*, allegory; and *sod*, mysticism.

The chief objective in study and prayer is to attach ourselves to the inner, spiritual, infinite light that is contained within the sacred words. Studying with this objective in mind is referred to by our Sages as "studying *lishmah*," for the sake of the Torah itself—for the sake of bonding with the infinite light that dwells within its words.

Regarding such study, R. Meir stated, "Whoever studies Torah *lishmah* merits many things and the Torah's secrets are revealed to him..." This means that—in addition to seeing the upper worlds—he is able to know the future and all events from within the Torah, and he is able to know how to conduct himself in his Divine service.

Entering the *pardeis* and appearing to be in the heavens means entering the actual words of Torah via the above approach, at which point the heavens—and everything else— are revealed.

FOCUS

Cherish sacred words
because G-d is within.

Responding to Hate

דֶער אַהֲבַת יִשְׂרָאֵל בֶּעדאַרף אוֹיף דִיר פּוֹעֵל זַיְין אַז דוּ זָאלְסְט נִיט
לָאזְן אַז עֶר זָאל טְרָאגְן אוֹיף זִיךְ אַ חֵטְא, אָבֶּער מִיט דֶעם וְוָאם
דוּ וֶועסְט אִים אוֹיסוְויְיזְן וְוִי דַיְין דֶרֶךְ אִיז גוּט אוּן דַיְין הַנְהָגָה
אִיז וְוִי עַל פִּי תּוֹרָה הַקְּדוֹשָׁה בֶּעדאַרף זַיְין, וְוֶעסְטוּ פוּן אִים
אַרָאפְּנֶעמֶען דֶעם חֵטְא פוּן "לא תִשְׂנָא אֶת אָחִיךְ בִּלְבָבֶךָ".

*Do not hate your brother in your heart; you shall surely rebuke
your brother, but do not incur a sin because of him* (Leviticus 19:17).

If one Jew hates another, even without acting upon it in
speech or action, he transgresses a prohibition. If a Jew hates
you, he is sinning, and you should perform *ahavat Yisrael* by
preventing him from hating you.

You shall surely rebuke your brother. The verb *hochei'ach*,
rebuke, also means prove, implying that you must proactively
approach the individual who hates you to discover the cause
of the problem. No doubt it has something to do with his
perception of your reverence for G-d; he believes you acted
contrary to the Torah. *Hochei'ach.* Prove yourself. Demonstrate
the innocence of your conduct.

If you did nothing wrong, why must you bear the burden of proof? For the Torah states: *Lo tisa alav cheit, do not incur a sin because of him.* This can be translated as: Do not cause a sin to be placed upon him. You have an obligation of *ahavat Yisrael,* which includes preventing others from sinning.

However, since you are in the right and have no need to justify yourself—and you are doing so simply for the sake of *ahavat Yisrael*—you might come across as insensitive or condescending. Here, the literal interpretation comes into play: *Do not incur a sin because of him*—if you needlessly humiliate or upset him, you will indeed incur a sin.

Hate is a mistake; be sensitive in correcting it.

A Prayer for Prayer

מָשָׁל שֶׁהִכְרִיז הַמֶּלֶךְ בְּיוֹם שִׂמְחָתוֹ כָּל מִי שֶׁיְבַקֵּשׁ דָּבָר מִן הַמֶּלֶךְ יְמַלְּאוּ לוֹ
בַּקָּשָׁתוֹ... וְהָיָה שָׁם חָכָם אֶחָד שֶׁאָמַר שֶׁשְּׁאֵלָתוֹ וּמְבַקָּשׁוֹ שֶׁיְּדַבֵּר הַמֶּלֶךְ
בְּעַצְמוֹ עִמּוֹ ג' פְּעָמִים בַּיוֹם, וְהוּטַב מְאֹד בְּעֵינֵי הַמֶּלֶךְ מֵאַחַר שֶׁדִּבּוּרוֹ
חָבִיב עָלָיו מִן עֹשֶׁר וְכָבוֹד, לָכֵן יְמַלֵּא בַּקָּשָׁתוֹ שֶׁיִּתְּנוּ לוֹ רְשׁוּת לְכָנֵס
בְּהֵיכָלוֹ לְדַבֵּר עִמּוֹ וְשָׁם יִפְתְּחוּ לוֹ הָאוֹצָרוֹת שֶׁיִּקַּח מִן עֹשֶׁר וְכָבוֹד גַּם
כֵּן. וְזֶהוּ שֶׁכָּתוּב "תְּפִלָּה לְעָנִי וגו' לִפְנֵי ה' יִשְׁפֹּךְ שִׂיחוֹ", שֶׁזֶּה מְבַקָּשׁוֹ.

There was once a king who announced on a grand day of personal celebration that whoever wishes to approach him with a personal request will have his wish granted. Indeed, they came—one seeking a position of authority and prestige, another requesting wealth, and so forth. The king granted these requests one after another.

Finally, an individual approached with an unusual appeal. He asked to be granted the honor of entering the palace and talking with the king himself three times each day. The king was mightily pleased with this request, because the man had asked for neither riches nor glory but for something far more precious in the beseecher's eyes—the opportunity to hold a dialogue with the king himself.

The monarch granted this request, and when the individual entered the palace thrice daily to speak with the king, the treasure houses of wealth and glory were opened before him so that he could take from them as well.

This is the deeper significance of the verse, *A prayer for a poor man when he enwraps himself and pours out his speech before G-d* (Psalms 102:1). What is his prayer? What does he request? Only that he be allowed to pour out his speech before G-d.

BEHAR

Sabbatical Living

"וְשָׁבְתָה הָאָרֶץ" — שְׁבִיתָה וּבִיטוּל אִין אֶרֶץ; מֶען
טְרָאגְט אַרַיְין שְׁבִיתָה אִין דִי עִנְיָנִים אַרְצִיִּים גוּפָא.

The earth shall rest as a Shabbat to G-d (Leviticus 25:2).

And now, Israel, what (mah) does G-d demand of you? Only to fear G-d… (Deuteronomy 10:12).

Shavsah, "rest," alludes to a state of bittul, submission and self-nullification before G-d. Aretz, "earth," alludes to our material affairs. Taken together, the verse offers us spiritual direction: ve-shavsah ha-aretz, let your material affairs experience submission to G-d. For it is within the power of each Jew to introduce a sense of nullification to G-d even in the material affairs of daily life.

The verse states, Only to fear G-d. The word only implies something simple, because once we achieve bittul, it is easy to fear G-d to a degree similar to Moses himself.

As our Sages comment on this verse, it is simple for a Jew to fear G-d, "because it comes readily to Moses." When they say Moses, they mean the state that he embodied. So "readily to Moses" means "readily to *bittul*," which easily brings us to the highest degrees of fearing G-d.

FOCUS

Extend your attachment and nullification before G-d to every part of your daily routine.

Two Virtues in One

'תַּלְמוּד גָּדוֹל שֶׁמֵּבִיא לִידֵי מַעֲשֶׂה'... כִּי תַלְמוּד יֵשׁ בּוֹ
שְׁנֵיהֶם, כִּי 'הָעוֹסֵק בְּתוֹרַת עוֹלָה כְּאִלּוּ הִקְרִיב עוֹלָה',
אִם כֵּן שְׁנֵיהֶם בְּיָדוֹ, מַה שֶּׁאֵין כֵּן מַעֲשֶׂה הוּא לְבָה.

The Sages debate whether study or practical deeds are superior. Their conclusion? "Study is greater, because it leads to action."

This statement is confusing. It insists that study is superior but argues that the superiority of study depends on something far more important: practical deeds.

The explanation: The superiority of study over action is that it includes both virtues. For our Sages taught that "whoever occupies himself with the study of the laws of the burnt-offering] is considered as having offered an actual burnt-offering." Consequently, the meaning of "study leads to action" is not that after one has studied he will then put it into practice. Rather, "study leads to action" at the very moment of study. For whatever subject he studies is considered as having been accomplished at that same moment.

In conclusion: Torah study includes action, whereas action— although the ultimate goal—does not include Torah study.

FOCUS

Your Torah study has powerful and instant results.

The Names of the Tribes

עֲנָוֶה פְּסוּלָה... רְאוּ מָה, וְכַוָּנָתוֹ רְאוּ שֶׁיֵּשׁ בִּי בְּחִינַת מָה, שֶׁהִיא
מִדַּת עֲנָוֶה... "רְאוּבֵן שִׁמְעוֹן לֵוִי יְהוּדָה", כְּמוֹ שֶׁיֵּשׁ שָׁמוֹת
הַשְּׁבָטִים בִּקְדֻשָּׁה כֵּן יֵשׁ בִּקְלִפָּה, וְהוּא, רְאוּבֵן רָאוּ שֶׁאֲנִי בֵּן,
שִׁמְעוֹן שֶׁעוֹשֶׂה הַטּוֹב כְּדֵי שֶׁיִּהְיֶה שָׁמְעוֹ בְּכָל הָעוֹלָם, לֵוִי שֶׁיִּתְחַבֵּר
לְאַנְשֵׁי מַעֲשֶׂה כְּדֵי יְהוּדָה, פֵּרוּשׁ שֶׁיּוֹדוּ וִישַׁבְּחוּ אוֹתוֹ.

The names of the twelve tribes allude to positive characteristics. However, if we lack genuine humility and submissiveness to G-d's will, our positive attributes can easily become perverted into negative traits. This is accomplished by the *yetzer hara* convincing us to engage in positive activities with ulterior, self-serving motives.

The name Reuven comes from *re'u ben* (See—a son!). The *yetzer hara* turns this into "See that *I am* a son!"—we desire that others see and take note of our accomplished status.

The name Shimon comes from *shama* (heard). The *yetzer hara* turns this into a desire for *sham'o*, his reputation—we want our good deeds to be widely publicized.

The name Levi comes from *lavah* (join). The *yetzer hara* causes us to desire that people attach our names to those whom society considers the distinguished elite.

The name Judah comes from *yodeh* (praise). This is turned into a desire to receive praise for our deeds.

If we work on ourselves to become truly humble—and not for the sake of being considered humble in the eyes of others— then we forestall the development of these negative tendencies, and the names can retain their original, sacred implications of characteristics that are purely for the sake of heaven.

FOCUS

Do good to be good, not to look good.

Doctor of Souls

"אִישׁ כִּי תִשְׂטֶה אִשְׁתּוֹ", שֶׁהוּא הַחֹמֶר וְהַגּוּף שֶׁעַל יָדוֹ נָטָה וְשָׂטָה
מִדֶּרֶךְ הַיָּשָׁר וְאֵינוֹ יוֹדֵעַ בְּאֵיזֶה דֶּרֶךְ יִבְחַר... אָז "וְהוּבָא אֶל הַכֹּהֵן",
שֶׁהֵם הַתַּלְמִידֵי חֲכָמִים רוֹפְאֵי הַנְּפָשׁוֹת. וְזֶהוּ שֶׁכָּתוּב "וְלָקַח הַכֹּהֵן"
מַיִם קְדוֹשִׁים, הֵם דִּבְרֵי תוֹרָה, "אֶל כְּלִי חֶרֶשׂ", רוֹצֶה לוֹמַר לְהַלְבִּישׁ
בְּמָשָׁל וּמְלִיצָה וְיֹאמַר לוֹ תּוֹכַחַת מוּסָר שֶׁיִּהְיֶה לוֹ רְפוּאָה.

*If a man's wife goes astray...he should bring his wife to the
kohen...The kohen should take sacred water in an earthen vessel,
and earth from the Tabernacle's floor...and put it into the water...*
(Numbers 5:12-17).

A body is the soul's wife, but its corporeal desires can lead us
astray:

The wicked are busy satisfying physical cravings, whereas a
tzaddik craves spirituality and shuns physicality by fasting and
the like. We must strike a careful balance between them:

We may imitate the *tzaddik*, but if we sense ourselves
growing weak or depressed, we must turn to the way of the

wicked—caring for our bodily needs, but solely for the sake of heaven. If we grow overly fond of the material path, we must shift towards the *tzaddik*'s abstinence and seriousness until we are out of danger.

If we do not strike the correct balance, our physicality has led us astray. We must seek a kohen—a Torah sage who is a doctor of souls. He will take sacred waters— the Torah's sublime teachings—and place them in earthen vessels, converting them into parables and explanations to which we can relate, tailoring his guidance to cure our particular ailments.

Serving as a doctor of souls is satisfying, which can lead to pride. The sage must take *"earth from the Tabernacle's floor"*—an extra dose of humility that he can *"put into the waters"*—offering Torah guidance with pure humility.

<table>
<tr><td>F O C U S</td><td>To stay fit in G-d's service,
find a spiritual trainer.</td></tr>
</table>

Born on a Summit

הָאָדָם נוֹלַד עַל זֶה הָהָר שֶׁהוּא הַגַּבְהוּת כְּמוֹ שֶׁאָמְרוּ חַזַ"ל
'הָאָדָם מִתְגָּאֶה עַל כֻּלָּם', וּלְפִיכָךְ דּוֹמֶה לוֹ שֶׁאֵין לוֹ גַּבְהוּת
וְאֵינוֹ בָּהָר כְּלָל, וְהַאֵיךְ יַבְחִין זֶה אִם לֹא שֶׁיֵּרֵד מִן הָהָר לְגַמְרֵי
לְרַגְלֵי הָהָר עַל הַבִּקְעָה מַמָּשׁ, דְּהַיְנוּ שֶׁיַּרְגִּיל אֶת עַצְמוֹ בִּכְנִיעָה
וְשִׁפְלוּת בְּלֵב וּבְמַעֲשֶׂה, וְהָעִקָּר בְּלֵב, וְיִתְוַדַּע לוֹ הָאֱמֶת.

A passenger dozed off as the wagon climbed a steep
mountain and rolled across a large plateau. He awoke, but he
refused to believe he was atop a mountain—it looked flat, and
he did not experience the climb. When the plateau ended and
the winding descent began, he realized he must have been on a
mountaintop after all.

We might not realize if we are perched atop an unholy
mountain, raising ourselves high above others in conceit. We
may consider ourselves wise, scholarly, with pedigree, wealthy,
of sterling character, perhaps even a *tzaddik* and one who
fears G-d—and pleasant and delightful to boot. We are above
everyone; it is beneath us to fraternize with others. We know

that trumpeting our own qualities too loudly will turn people off, so we add "humility" to our list of superiorities. After all, if we are gracious enough to fraternize with others, are we not quite humble?

We cannot recognize our own arrogance, because we never experienced the climb. We were born on a summit, gifted with a natural dose of arrogance. When we begin life atop a mountain, we are incapable of seeing our true position—until we descend. By actively working on lowering ourselves with genuine humility before others and recognizing the supreme greatness of our Creator, which makes all humans equally insignificant, we begin to recognize our mountain for what it is. We must descend all the way to the valley by acting consistently with genuine humility, and more critically, by developing a genuinely humble heart.

FOCUS Seek ways to see yourself accurately.

The Divine Kiss

הָאָדָם רָאוּי לָשׂוּם לֵב וְלוֹמַר כִּי הוּא "סֻלָּם מֻצָּב אַרְצָה וְרֹאשׁוֹ מַגִּיעַ הַשָּׁמַיְמָה", וְכָל תְּנוּעוֹתָיו וַעֲסָקָיו וְדִבּוּרוֹ [וְהִלּוּכוֹ] עוֹשֶׂה רוֹשֶׁם לְמַעְלָה [לְמַעְלָה], בְּוַדַּאי יִזָּהֵר בְּכָל דְּרָכָיו וַעֲסָקָיו שֶׁיִּהְיֶה לְשֵׁם שָׁמַיִם.

Excessive humility is an obstacle, fooling us into believing that we do not draw Divine light to all the worlds through our prayer and study—whereas in truth even the angels are sustained from our efforts.

Believing that we are too insignificant to damage or improve the heavens or the earth leads to anarchy without oversight. Rather, we must recognize that we bond with G-d Himself with each positive deed we do.

If we would recognize our power, we would throw ourselves into G-d's service with tremendous joy; we would be in awe of our good fortune. We would be scrupulous with our every movement and word, paying attention to the statement of King David: *If you lie between the borders* (Psalms 68:14)—the word *shefatayim*, borders, is related to *sefatayim*, lips. G-d waits and watches our lips, eager to kiss them when we pronounce words of Torah and prayer with love and awe. Who can contemplate this thought without trembling? The great and awesome King of the universe is waiting and watching the lips of a truly lowly human!

Excessive humility undermines all this. Remember: We are ladders with feet on the earth and heads in the heavens. Our every movement and word influences the heavens. Surely we will ensure that our every activity is performed for the sake of heaven.

FOCUS

More than you look to G-d,
G-d looks eagerly to you.

Double Standards

קֹרַח עַל עַצְמוֹ לֹא דִּמָּה שֶׁיִּהְיֶה לוֹ גַבְהוּת, רַק חָשַׁב שֶׁמַּה שֶׁלִּבּוֹ
נוֹטֶה לְזֶה לִהְיוֹת נָשִׂיא הַכֹּל הוּא מִצַּד הָאֱמֶת, כַּנַּ"ל בַּפָּסוּק "וַיִּגְבַּה
לִבּוֹ בְּדַרְכֵי ה'", כִּי זֹאת הַגַּאֲוָה הֻתְּרָה, וְלֹא רָצָה לִתְלוֹת הַפְּחִיתוּת
בּוֹ בְּגַבְהוּתוֹ הָאָסוּר, וּכְאֶמֶת הַיּוֹשֶׁר שֶׁל הַגַּבְהוּת הַמֻּתָּר הוּא בְּמשֶׁה,
רַק חָשַׁב לְהֵפֶךְ מִפְּנֵי הַקִּנְאָה שֶׁל הָרָע שֶׁהָפַךְ לִבּוֹ לֵאמֹר עַל רַע
טוֹב וְעַל טוֹב רָע, וְלֹא הֶאֱמִין שֶׁמִּפִּי הַדִּבּוּר עָשָׂה משֶׁה הַכֹּל.

Moses was entirely humble, but as a Jewish king tasked with training his nation to serve G-d, he demonstrated strength of leadership. Despite Korah's brilliance and Divine inspiration, he failed to appreciate this balance, arguing: *Why do you raise yourselves above G-d's community?* (Numbers 16:3). Rashi explains: "You took far more than enough greatness for yourselves!"

In other words, at the outset of a mitzvah, a measure of self-promotion is permitted if it is indispensable to motivating us. However, once we are successfully engaged in the mitzvah, and certainly after completing it, we must shed every trace of pride.

Korah consented that since Moses hesitated to become the leader as G-d commanded, he required a boost from self-promotion, but only just enough to get going. He considered Moses' continued strength of command "far more than enough."

Korah harbored a trace of jealousy that stemmed from arrogance, which led him to an incorrect assumption: He projected his own blemish onto Moses, assuming that Moses' conduct was the result of arrogance and not strictly according to G-d's command. He considered himself humble, seeking leadership solely for G-d's sake, in the spirit of, *His heart was uplifted in the ways of G-d* (II Chronicles 17:6). His jealousy led him to confuse good and bad.

Moses responded, *It is enough for you, sons of Levi!* (Numbers 16:7). You consider your self-promotion Divine, and mine, evil. *Rav lachem* (It is enough for you) can be read as *rav,* the greatness you seek, *lachem*, is for you, for your sakes, not for G-d's sake.

FOCUS

The flaws you see in others may just be your own.

A Perplexing Law

הַגַּבְהוּת בִּשְׁעַת מַעֲשֵׂה הַמִּצְוָה שֶׁאָז הוּא נִקְרָא טָהוֹר, וְאָז הַגַּבְהוּת
מְטַמֵּא טְהוֹרִים חַם וְשָׁלוֹם, וְהַגַּבְהוּת נִקְרָא 'פָּרָה' — שֶׁמַּפְרָה וּמַגְדִּיל
דַּעַת הָאָדָם... וְנִקְרָא זֶה פָּרָה אֲדָמָה הַמְטַהֶרֶת אֶת הַטְּמֵאִים.

The word *parah*, cow, also means to increase or proliferate.
Adumah, red, is symbolic of *kelipah*, the forces of evil. Taken
together, the term *parah adumah* (red cow) alludes to
inappropriate inflation of self-worth that results in the evil trait
of arrogance.

A puzzling feature of the laws governing *parah adumah*
is that the process purifies the ritually impure but transmits
impurity to the pure.[1] In spiritual terms, arrogance can bring
purity to those who need spiritual cleansing, but it is destructive
to those who are advanced in the service of G-d.

---

1. The cow is slaughtered and then burned in the precise manner described in the
Torah. Its ashes are mixed with water and sprinkled upon a person who is severely
impure from contact with a corpse. That individual is thereby restored to purity. However, those preparing the ashes gain a limited degree of impurity in the process.

We should not serve G-d for personal gain or considerations, however subtle; we should do what G-d desires simply because that is His will. Studying or doing a mitzvah to earn reward in heaven is considered self-serving for those who are advanced in their service. It is arrogant, disqualifies their service, and introduces spiritual impurity to the pure.

The reverse is true of those unfamiliar with G-d's service. They cannot ignore all enticements, such as heavenly rewards, because they may otherwise be unmotivated to serve G-d. They must invite a measure of haughtiness—a self-serving motivation—to facilitate the move from impurity to purity.

FOCUS

Use pride as an umbrella; fold it up once you get inside.

Treasured Nation

אידֶען, וֶוער זֵיי זָאלֶען ניט זֵיין, אַלט און יונג, מֶענֶער און פֿרויֶען, פֿרום
און פֿריי, און אין וֶועלכֶען פּלַאץ עֶס זָאל ניט זֵיין הָאבֶען זֵיי דֶעם
אויבֶּערשטֶען גלויבֶּען — אֱמוּנָה — און ליבשַאפֿט — אַהֲבָה
— און פֿורכט — יִרְאָה — אוֹצְרוֹת צו און פֿאַר אונזֶער ליבֶּען ג-ט
בָּרוּך הוּא, נָאר מֶען בַּאדַארף דָאס מיט גרויס מיה אויפֿדֶעקֶן, אָט
אַזוי ווי מֶען דֶעקֶט אויף די טיף אין דֶער עֶרד בַּאהַאלטֶענֶע אוֹצְרוֹת.

....

Who can count the dust of Jacob? (Numbers 23:10)

This verse teaches us that the Jews are compared to soil.
Similarly, G-d declared, *You shall be for Me a desirable land*
(Malachi 3:12).

The earth contains the greatest treasures: metals, water,
etc. The full extent of its treasures lies undiscovered and will be
discovered with time. This is especially true of the ability that
G-d gave the earth to produce and thereby sustain all creatures.

We all tread on the earth, but we all need its products of
food and water. However, we must dig deep to uncover its
treasures, and we must plow and plant to reap its produce.

By nature, Jews are treasure houses of inborn faith and love for G-d. We contain the greatest treasures of morals and wisdom. In comparison to all other nations, we produce wisdom and scientific discoveries, disproportionately to our small numbers.

Just as all trample the earth but need it during their lifetimes and after their deaths, so does humanity trample the Jews— but they all need us. Each Jew, old or young, man or woman, religious or otherwise, harbors the treasures of faith, love, and awe for our beloved G-d. Serious effort must be invested in uncovering these treasures, similar to the effort required to reach untapped treasures beneath thick layers of soil.

FOCUS

Dig deep, uncover your light, be a lantern for your surroundings.

Holy Jokers

"יִפְקֹד ה' ... אִישׁ... וַאֲשֶׁר יוֹצִיאֵם, וַאֲשֶׁר יְבִיאֵם", כִּי רֹאשׁ הַדּוֹר יוּכַל
לְהַעֲלוֹת כָּל הַדִּבּוּרִים וְהַסִפּוּרִים שֶׁל אַנְשֵׁי דוֹרוֹ, לְקַשֵּׁר הַגַּשְׁמִי בְּרוּחָנִי.

Let G-d appoint a man over the congregation ... who will take
them out and bring them in... (Numbers 27:16-17).

People tend to fill their years with a vast amount of chatter,
idle talk, sharing stories and tidbits, and similar mundane
speech.

The spiritual leader of a generation has the ability to elevate
all this mundane speech. He can *take them out and bring them*
in; meaning, he can take the speech out of its mundane state
and bring it into the realm of sanctity.

He accomplishes this by connecting their mundane
exchanges with the realm of sanctity in a manner similar to
the case of the two jesters described in the Talmud in Tractate
Ta'anit. The jesters deliberately employed light banter for the

sake of heaven, telling jokes to depressed people to lighten their mood and restore a measure of optimism. In doing so, these jesters were able to elevate the mundane conversations of the people they encountered.

FOCUS

Even the casual conversation of a *tzaddik* is elevating.

Divinity Conductor

בִּכְדֵי אוֹיף צוּקוּמֶען צוּ דֶעם רָצוֹן וֶואָם אִיז בְּמַתָּנָה בַּא יֶעדֶערָן, הוּא
עַל יְדֵי "לְשַׁכֵּן שְׁמוֹ שָׁם" — מוֹסֵר נֶפֶשׁ זַיִין זִיךְ לְפַרְסֵם אֱלֹקוּתוֹ בָּעוֹלָם.
וֶואָם אִיז דֶער מְסִירַת נֶפֶשׁ אִין דֶעם — מִיט אַ בְּרָכָה וּפָסוּק תְּהִלִּים.

*When you come into the land...take of the first of all the fruit
of the ground...and go to the place that G-d will choose to have His
Name dwell there* (Deuteronomy 26:2).

Aretz, land, is associated with *ratzon*, desire. How can you
"come into the desire"—earn the experience of a genuine G-dly
desire and spiritual satisfaction? *Go to the place that G-d will
choose to have His Name dwell there*—through practicing self-

sacrifice for the sake of making Divinity dwell in your physical location. With what is this self-sacrifice expressed? With the recital of a blessing or a verse from Psalms.

G-d put you where you are so that you can bring Him there through a blessing or verse of Psalms.

Life Journeys

דִי מ"ב מַסָּעוֹת... זַיינֶען אַלֶע פַאראַן בַּיי יֶעדֶער אִידֶן, בְּמֶשֶׁךְ שְׁנוֹת
חַיָּיו: "אֲשֶׁר יָצְאוּ מֵאֶרֶץ מִצְרַיִם" — לֵידַת הָאָדָם, דֶּערְנָאךְ בְּמֶשֶׁךְ
יְמֵי חַיָּיו — שְׁאָר הַמַּסָּעוֹת, בִּיז עֶר קוּמְט צוּ אֶרֶץ הַחַיִּים הָעֶלְיוֹנָה.

These are the journeys of the children of Israel when they left the land of Egypt (Numbers 33:1).

The Torah lists forty-two journeys from Egypt to the Holy Land. In a sense, these same forty-two journeys are undertaken by each Jew during his lifetime. Our journey begins with leaving Egypt, which alludes to childbirth—the first step of our sojourn on earth. Our remaining steps play out during the course of our lifetime until we reach our final destination.

Our last step is to enter the supernal Land of Life.

The events and conditions that shape your life are highly orchestrated.

Appreciating Jews

"שָׁמוֹעַ בֵּין אֲחֵיכֶם", "שָׁמוֹעַ" דֶער וָואס הָאט אַ חוּש הַשְׁמִיעָה רוּחָני
אוּן הֶערט אוֹים ווי גרוֹים ס׳אִיז די אַהֲבַת הַשֵּׁם בָּרוּךְ הוּא צוּ יֶעדֶער אִידֶן,
ווי יֶעדֶער אִיד אִיז טַייעֶר לְמַעֲלָה, דֶער אִיד אִיז "בֵּין אֲחֵיכֶם", 'בֵּין׳
לְשׁוֹן הֲבָנָה, אָט דֶער פַארְשְׁטֵייט די גרוֹיסקַייט פוּן אַ אִידְן... אִיז
"בֵּין אֲחֵיכֶם", עֶר אִיז אוֹיסגֶעבּוּנְדֶן מִיט אִידְן אוּן פִילְט אַ עוֹנֶג רוּחָני
אִין אוּן פוּן יֶעדְן אִידְן בַּאזוּנְדֶער... בִּכְדֵי דֶער מֶענְטשׁ זָאל קָרִיגְן
אַ חוּשׁ הַשְׁמִיעָה רוּחָני, דֶערְהֶערן אוּן דֶערְפִילְן די גרוֹיסקַייט פוּן
אַ אִידְן, אִיז "בֵּין אֲחֵיכֶם", אִיז נָאר ווֶען מֶען אִיז אוֹיסְגֶעבּוּנְדֶן מִיט
אִידְן, אוּן אַלֶע אִידְן אֲפִילוּ די גָאר פְּשׁוּטֶ׳ע זַיינֶען זַיינֶע אַחִים.

Hear between your brothers and judge justly between a man and his brother (Deuteronomy 1:16).

This command lends itself to three spiritual interpretations:

1. *Shamoa*, hear, refers to a person blessed with a spiritual sense of hearing. He "hears between his brothers," meaning that he perceives the magnitude of G-d's love towards each and every Jew. He perceives the preciousness of

each Jew in G-d's eyes. A Jew with such sensitivity can be described as *bein acheichem, between your brothers*. The word *bein* (between) is related to *binah*, understanding. He understands the greatness of his brethren.

2. A person endowed with this spiritual sense of hearing is *between your brothers*—he is literally within his fellow Jews. He is connected with his fellow Jews to the point that he feels the spiritual pleasure that is within and that emanates from each Jew individually.

3. The method by which to acquire this spiritual sense of hearing is *bein acheichem*, through genuinely connecting with your brethren. All Jews, even the most simple, are truly your siblings. Such an approach is the only way to gain this inner appreciation.

FOCUS

If you love Jews enough, you'll understand why.

A Teacher's Gift

"וְשִׁנַּנְתָּם", דוּ זָאלְסְט מְשַׁנֵן זַיִין, לְשׁוֹן שִׁינוּן, "לְבָנֶיךָ", צוּ דִי וָואס
וְוילְן פַארְשְׁטֵיין, "וְדִבַּרְתָּ בָּם", זָאלְסְט אַרַיְינְרֶעדֶן אִין זֵיי, דוּרְךְ
דֶעם וֶועט זַיִין "בְּשִׁבְתְּךָ בְּבֵיתֶךָ", דִי אֵייגֶענֶע נִיצוֹצוֹת מְבַרֵר זַיִין,
"וּבְלֶכְתְּךָ בַדֶּרֶךְ", מְבַרֵר זַיִין אִין יֶענֶעם אוּן אִין עוֹלָם, דָאס אִיז
נוֹגֵעַ "וּבְשָׁכְבְּךָ" — יוֹם הַמִּיתָה, "וּבְקוּמֶךָ" — תְּחִיַת הַמֵּתִים.

Teach them thoroughly to your children; discuss them while sitting in your home, while you walk on the road, when you lie down, and when you arise. (Deuteronomy 6:7)

The word *ve-shinantam* (*teach them thoroughly*) comes from *shinun*, to repeatedly review a subject until it is completely clear. *To your children* refers to those who wish to understand. *Vedibarta bam* (*discuss them*) can be translated literally as speak into them, so that your teachings penetrate your students.

The result of your diligence will be *sitting in your home*—your disciples will be empowered to elevate their "home," meaning their personal sparks of G-dliness. *While you walk on the road—*

they will be successful in elevating others as well as their environment, which will be especially relevant to you *when you lie down*—after a person's passing, when he reaps the rewards of his efforts, *and when you arise*—in the ultimate era of reward, the era of the Resurrection.

FOCUS

Share wisdom; you will receive more than you give.

A Sage Leads Us to G-d

וְזֶהוּ שֶׁכָּתוּב 'אֵין, לְגַבֵּי מֹשֶׁה זוּטַרְתִּי', רוֹצֶה לוֹמַר: מֵאַחַר שֶׁכְּבָר נִכְנְסוּ
בִּירְאַת תַּלְמִידֵי חֲכָמִים שֶׁהִיא 'לְגַבֵּי מֹשֶׁה', שֶׁנֶּאֱמַר "וַיִּירְאוּ מִגֶּשֶׁת
אֵלָיו", אִם כֵּן, 'זוּטַרְתִּי' לָבוֹא גַם כֵּן לְיִרְאַת ה', שֶׁזֶּה נִמְשָׁךְ מִזֶּה.

What does G-d demand of you? Only to fear G-d...
(Deuteronomy 10:12).

"Only" implies something relatively simple, leading to our Sages' question: "Is fearing G-d a small accomplishment?" They respond, "Yes, for Moses it *is* a small matter."

Many have questioned the meaning of this response, because, after all, the verse is addressed to all Jews and not exclusively to Moses. But first, let us examine another verse: *You shall fear G-d* (Deuteronomy 6:13). Our Sages state that this includes reverence for Torah sages.

The Maharsha explains the appropriateness of this association: When one is in awe of a Torah sage, then even if he is utterly unlearned, he will come to fear G-d as well.

This clarifies our original verse as well: The Jews were in awe of Moses, as it says, *They were afraid to approach him* (Exodus 34:30). Since they experienced the fear of a Torah sage, it was easy for them to extend that feeling to a fear of G-d. "For Moses it *is* a small matter" means that because they had awe "for Moses," it was therefore "a small matter" to arrive at a fear for G-d.

FOCUS

Broaden your awe of G-d through anecdotes of our sages and *tzaddikim.*

Know Your Worth

רֹב עַנְוְתָנוּתוֹ שֶׁל הָאָדָם גּוֹרֵם שֶׁנִּתְרַחֵק מֵעֲבוֹדַת הַשֵּׁם יִתְבָּרֵךְ,
שֶׁמִּצַּד שְׁפְלוּתוֹ אֵינוֹ מַאֲמִין כִּי הָאָדָם גּוֹרֵם עַל יְדֵי תְּפִלָּתוֹ וְתוֹרָתוֹ
שֶׁפַע אֶל כָּל הָעוֹלָמוֹת, וְגַם הַמַּלְאָכִים נִזּוֹנִין עַל יְדֵי תּוֹרָתוֹ וּתְפִלָּתוֹ.
שֶׁאִלּוּ הָיָה מַאֲמִין זֶה כַּמָּה הָיָה עוֹבֵד ה' בְּשִׂמְחָה וּבְיִרְאָה מֵרֹב
כֹּל, וְהָיָה נִזְהָר בְּכָל אוֹת וּתְנוּעָה וּמִלָּה לְאָמְרָהּ כִּדְקָא יָאוּת.

*So that G-d may...grant you compassion and be compassionate
with you* (Deuteronomy 13:18).

Grant you compassion refers to our *ability* to be
compassionate. The phrase *be compassionate with you* implies
that as a result of our compassionate acts, G-d showers us with
overt compassion, because G-d mirrors our deeds. When we
exercise a particular attribute, G-d activates His corresponding
attribute.

It is important to realize this in order to be properly
motivated in Divine service. If we believe our mortal deeds have
no influence in heaven, we will not bother to serve G-d. This is
humility taken to an unhealthy extreme, similar to our Sages'

statement, "The humility of R. Zechariah caused the [Temple's] destruction." It leads to a complete lack of accountability.

The truth is that every mortal thought, word, or deed reverberates loudly in heaven. If they are positive, they sustain the angels, illuminate the heavens, and provide G-d with the satisfaction He eagerly awaits.

If we truly understood this, we would throw ourselves eagerly into G-d's service and carefully weigh every move and thought.

FOCUS

If you seek G-d's compassion,
show compassion to others.

SHOFTIM

Heart of Fire

תַּלְמִידֵי חֲכָמִים וְועלְכֶע לֶערנֶען תּוֹרָה זַיינֶען אש... אָבֶּער דָאם אִיז
נִיט כִּי "אֵינֶנּוּ אָכָל", וַויִיל דִי תַּלְמִידֵי חֲכָמִים זַיינֶען מְרַוֶּה זֵיעֶר אש
מִיט דִי חִדּוּשֵׁי תּוֹרָה וְועלְכֶע זֵיי זַיינֶען מְחַדֵּשׁ. אָבֶּער דֶער סְנֶה, דִי
אֲנָשִׁים פְּשׁוּטִים, וָואם אִין זֵיי אִיז דֶער לַבַּת אש דִי הַארץ פוּן פֵּייעֶר,
בָּא זֵיי מִיט זֵיעֶר עֶרנְסְטֶע תְּמִימוּת'דִיקֶע תְּפִלּוֹת אוּן תְּהִלִּים זָאגן
הַגַּם דְּלָא יָדְעֵי מַאי קָאמְרֵי אָבֶּער וַויִיל דָאם קוּמְט פוּן דֶער אֱמוּנָה
פְּשׁוּטָה, אִיז דֶער לַבַּת אש אֵינֶנּוּ אָכָל, דָאם וֶוערְט קֵיינְמָאל נִיט
גֶעשְׁטִילְט אוּן זֵיי הָאבְּן אַ תְּשׁוּקָה צוּ גֶ־טְלֶעכְקֵייט אוּן תּוֹרָה אוּן מִצְוֹת.

*An angel of G-d appeared to him in a flame of fire from within
the thorn bush, and behold, the thorn bush was burning with fire,
but the thorn bush was not being consumed* (Exodus 3:2).

The Torah compares mortals to trees, but there are various
kinds of trees. A Torah scholar is a fruit-bearing tree. A thorn
bush represents those lacking any spiritual achievement.

Torah scholars are aflame with Divine fire, because the
Torah is spiritual fire, but it can easily burn itself out when their

passion for G-dliness is quenched by the satisfaction of spiritual accomplishments due to the novel Torah insights they uncover.

By contrast, the passionate thirst for G-dliness experienced by ordinary, unlearned Jews is compared to the fire in the thorn bush that is never consumed. The Torah describes it as *labat eish*, "a flame of fire," but *labat* comes from the word *leiv*, heart. Ordinary Jews have hearts of fire; their sincere and simple prayers and recital of Psalms—despite their unfamiliarity with the meaning of the phrases they recite—flow forth with pure and uncomplicated faith. Their hearts of fire are never consumed, meaning that their passion never wavers, because they lack the satisfaction of spiritual accomplishments that the Torah scholars enjoy. Instead, they are constantly aflame with yearning for G-dliness, for Torah and *mitzvot*.

FOCUS

G-d seeks a passionate relationship with you.

Fluctuations in
Divine Marriage

בְּג' דְרָכִים, א' בְּכֶסֶף, בְּחִינַת חֶסֶד, יְמֵי הַחֶסֶד שֶׁהַקָּדוֹשׁ בָּרוּךְ הוּא מַסִּיעוֹ
בְּחַסְדוֹ הַגָּדוֹל בַּתְּחִלָּה וְאָז כּוֹסֵף וְחוֹשֵׁק וּמִתְלַהֵב בְּתוֹרָתוֹ וַעֲבוֹדָתוֹ
יִתְבָּרֵךְ... בִּשְׁטָר שֶׁהֵם אוֹתִיּוֹת הַכְּתוּבִים בְּסֵפֶר שֶׁנִּקְרָא שְׁטָר, בֵּין
בְּאוֹתִיּוֹת הַתּוֹרָה בְּלִמּוּדוֹ, וּבֵין בַּתְּפִלָּה... עַד שֶׁיַּחְזוֹר אַחַר כַּךְ לְהִתְעַנֵּג
בּוֹ יִתְבָּרֵךְ עַל יְדֵי שֶׁבָּאוּ הַמּוֹחִין בַּתּוֹרָה וּתְפִלָּה שֶׁנִּקְרָא בְּבִיאָה.

The relationship between G-d and the Jewish people is often depicted as a marriage, whereby G-d is our Husband and we are His wife. Our Sages list the three methods for a man to take a woman as his wife: With *kesef*, an exchange of money [or an item of value such as a ring]; with *shtar*, a written deed (marriage contract); and with *bi'ah*, marital relations.

In the marriage between G-d and the Jewish people, all three are present: *Kesef*, money, is related to *kosef*, longing or yearning. *Kesef* symbolizes *chessed*, kindness. In the initial days of our attraction to Divine service, G-d in His great kindness assists us by providing us with inspiration so that we long, yearn, and are passionate about studying Torah, praying, and serving Him.

Then the wonder departs and our inspiration fizzles. We no longer experience a yearning for Divine service. Nevertheless, we are bound to Him through the power of the *shtar*, the written contract. We apply ourselves to the written words of Torah and prayer even if the appropriate feelings elude us, because the mere words of our contract with G-d have a power of their own.

Eventually, through our persistent efforts, we return to a state in which we derive great pleasure from our relationship with G-d, when we enter the Torah and prayers with reawakened minds. This entry into the significance of the words we study and recite is considered *bi'ah* (literally, entry), restored marital relations with G-d.

FOCUS

When your inspiration fizzles, persist.
It will rebound far stronger.

Baskets of Fruit

"וְהָלַכְתָּ אֶל הַמָּקוֹם" — הוּא עִנְיַן הַשְׁגָּחָה פְּרָטִית, "אֲשֶׁר יִבְחַר ה'
אֱלֹקֶיךָ" — אַז אַ אִיד גֵּייט אִין אַן אָרְט, אִיז דָאם נִיט וָואם עֶר גֵּייט
נָאר מְ'פִירְט אִיהם, דִי הַשְׁגָּחָה הָעֶלְיוֹנָה. אִיז אַז עֶר קוּמְט אִין אַן
אָרְט אִיז דִי כַּוָּנָה, "לְשַׁכֵּן שְׁמוֹ שָׁם" — לְפַרְסֵם אֱלֹקוּת בָּעוֹלָם.

*When you enter the land that G-d gives you as an inheritance,
and you possess and settle it, take the first of all the fruit of the
ground that you will bring from your land that G-d is giving you,
put them in a basket, and go to the place that G-d will choose to
make His Name dwell there* (Deuteronomy 26:2).

Aretz, land, is related to *ratzon*, will, as our Sages state,
"Why is the earth called *aretz*? Because it desires to perform its
Creator's will."

When you enter the land—when you arrive at a powerful
desire for spirituality, you must realize *that G-d is giving you* the
ability to experience this yearning, because He bequeathed it
to each Jew as a gift. *You possess and settle it*—it is your duty to
internalize the experience so that it settles permanently within
you.

Take of the first of all the fruit...put them in a basket—Divine lights must be captured with appropriate receptacles; spiritual highs must be tethered to daily reality by translating them into practical deeds.

How is this done? *Go to the place that G-d will choose.* When we travel to a specific location, it is not us who chose to journey there; rather, Divine Providence orchestrated events leading us to the location that requires elevation through our Divine service.

What is the nature of that service? *To make His Name dwell there*—to spread Divinity throughout the physical world.

FOCUS

G-d has provided you with a mission, destination, and inspiration.

Moving Closer

מֹשֶׁה רַבֵּינוּ הָאט פַארְשְׁטַאנֶען דִי מַחֲזֶה הָעֶלְיוֹנָה, וְואם מֶען בַּאוַוייזְט
אִים דִי מַעֲלָה הַגְּדוֹלָה פוּן אֲנָשִׁים פְּשׁוּטִים לְגַבֵּי תַּלְמִידֵי חֲכָמִים,
אַז דֶער לַהַט אֵשׁ אִיז נָאר אִין סְנֶה, אִיז עֶר גֶעקוּמֶען צוּ דֶער דַרְגָּא
פוּן תְּשׁוּבָה, נָאר לִהְיוֹת מֹשֶׁה רַבֵּינוּ אִיז דָאךְ גֶעוֶוען אַ צַדִּיק גָּמוּר,
וְואם דֶער אוֹפֶן הַתְּשׁוּבָה פוּן אַ צַדִּיק גָּמוּר אִיז בְּאוֹפֶן אַחֵר וְוי דִי
גֶעוֶוייְנְלֶעכֶע תְּשׁוּבָה, בַּא לֵידַת מֹשֶׁה רַבֵּינוּ זָאגְט דִי תּוֹרָה "וַתֵּרֶא
אוֹתוֹ כִּי טוֹב הוּא' — שֶׁנִּתְמַלֵּא הַבַּיִת כֻּלּוֹ אוֹרָה", אִיז זַיין אוֹפֶן
תְּשׁוּבָה — 'אָסוּרָה מִכַּאן לְהִתְקָרֵב לְשָׁם', וְואם דִי כַּוָּנָה אִיז אַז
מֶען בַּאדַארְף זִיךְ נִיט מִסְתַּפֵּק זַיין מִיט דֶעם מַעֲמָד וּמַצָּב וְואם מֶען
שְׁטֵייט, אֲפִילוּ אַ צַדִּיק גָּמוּר וְוי מֹשֶׁה רַבֵּינוּ דַארְף הָאבְּן דִי עֲבוֹדָה פוּן
'אָסוּרָה מִכַּאן לְהִתְקָרֵב לְשָׁם', וְואם דָאם אִיז דִי תְּנוּעָה פוּן תְּשׁוּבָה.

When Moses encountered the thorn bush, he exclaimed, *Let me turn now and see this great vision. Why does the thorn bush not burn up?* (Exodus 3:3). Rashi explains the opening phrase, *Let me turn now,* as follows: Let me turn away from here in order to draw closer to there.

Moses understood the vision: Fiery passion for G-d is not the hallmark of Torah scholars, but of simple, unlearned Jews who are compared to a thorn bush for lack of spiritual accomplishment. Moses was struck by this superiority of the ordinary Jew over the Torah scholar, and he was inspired to a state of *teshuvah* (repentance).

Moses was a complete *tzaddik*, and his *teshuvah* was not like that of ordinary people. After all, when he was born, his mother *saw that he was good* (Exodus 2:2), which means that "the house filled entirely with luminance." Rather, Moses' *teshuvah* was specifically in the manner of "Let me turn away from here in order to draw closer to there."

The message of this phrase is that we can never be satisfied with our current spiritual accomplishments. Even a complete *tzaddik* such as Moses must fulfill the Divine mission of constantly turning away from his current achievements in order to draw ever closer and achieve even more. This is the essence of *teshuvah*.

FOCUS

Don't believe in plateaus; keep climbing.

VAYEILECH

In the Dark

דער פֵּירוּש פֿוּן "הַסְתֵּר אַסְתִּיר" — צְװֵײ מָאל הַסְתֵּר — אִיז, אַז
דער הֶסְתֵּר גוּפֿא אִיז פֿאַרבָּאַרגְן. דָאס הֵייסְט אַז דֶער פֿאַרשְׁטֶעל
אִיז אַזוֹי גְרוֹיס, אַז מֶען פִּילְט גָאָרנִיט אַז דָאס אִיז אַ הֶסְתֵּר בִּיז
אַז עֶם קָאן קוּמֶען חַס וְשָׁלוֹם צוּ — "שָׁמַיִם חֹשֶׁךְ לְאוֹר".

Hide, I shall hide My face on that day (Deuteronomy 31:18).

The emphasis implied by the repetition of hide indicates
that the concealment of G-d's presence in this world is *itself*
concealed. In other words, when the spiritual darkness grows
too powerful, you stop realizing that it is darkness, and you can,
G-d forbid, mistake it for goodness and light.

Imagine yourself at the base of a spiral staircase. Look up,
see the image at its very top. Start ascending, keeping an eye on
that final destination. As you proceed, a supporting pillar blocks
your view. In truth, you have moved closer than before, but
because your destination has suddenly disappeared from your

sight, you might think you are at a greater distance from your destination.

Do not be fooled. Between one achievement and the next, you must move around a pole that produces momentary obstructions of vision, but as long as you are climbing, you are moving closer, not further.

FOCUS

Seek methods of ensuring
your path remains true.

HA'AZINU

To See and to Be Seen

וְזֶהוּ מַדְרֵגָה גְדוֹלָה לְאָדָם שֶׁיִּרְאֶה תָּמִיד בְּעֵין שִׂכְלוֹ הַשֵּׁם
יִתְבָּרֵךְ כְּמוֹ שֶׁמִּסְתַּכֵּל עַל אָדָם אֶחָד, וְיַחְשׁוֹב שֶׁגַּם הַבּוֹרֵא
יִתְבָּרֵךְ מִסְתַּכֵּל עָלָיו כְּמוֹ אָדָם אַחֵר שֶׁמִּסְתַּכֵּל עָלָיו, כָּל זֶה
יִהְיֶה תָּמִיד בְּמַחֲשַׁבְתּוֹ וּבְמַחֲשָׁבָה זַכָּה וּבְרוּרָה וּצְלוּלָה.

Here is an exceptionally great goal to work towards:

Constantly see G-d with your mind's eye in the same
manner that you gaze at your fellow humans with your physical
eyes. At the same time, contemplate that G-d is gazing at you
in turn, and that He is doing so with at least the same clarity
and intensity with which a mortal gazes at a person who stands

before him. All this should be kept constantly in your thoughts, and it should be crystal clear and real.

FOCUS

Keep reminding yourself of G-d's intimate presence.

Diligence in Study

"וְרוּחַ אֱלֹהִים מְרַחֶפֶת", דְּהַיְנוּ רוּחוֹ שֶׁל אָדָם, שֶׁיְרַחֵף
עַל פְּנֵי הַמַּיִם, הִיא הַתּוֹרָה, "וַיֹּאמֶר ה' יְהִי אוֹר", רוֹצֶה
לוֹמַר: שֶׁיָּאִיר ה' עֵינָיו עַל יְדֵי אוֹר הַתּוֹרָה.

*The spirit of G-d was hovering upon the surface of the waters.
And G-d said: Let there be light!* (Genesis 1:2-3).

You have the spirit of G-d within you. It is your soul. When
you invest your very soul into studying the Torah—the Divine
waters—hovering with patience and diligence over its sacred
words, attempting to reach greater depths of insight, then G-d
commands, *Let there be light!*—you will suddenly find your eyes
illuminated with the light of the Torah.

King David prayed, *Do not cast me aside in old age!* (Psalms 71:9).

This is the cry of the Torah to each Jew: Do not treat my teachings as old material!

View me as new each day!

Pay Up

אֲנַחְנוּ מַכְרִיזִין בַּשׁוֹפָר ל׳ יוֹם לְהָבִיא הַכֶּסֶף
לְשַׁלֵם בְּרֹאשׁ הַשָּׁנָה וּבְיוֹם הַכִּפּוּרִים.

There was once a creditor and a debtor. For thirty days, the creditor issued daily warnings—he would seize the debtor's land if payment was not forthcoming. He hoped the debtor would be frightened into paying his debt. The debtor was indeed concerned, but, unable to secure the funds, he paid his debt with fake coins. He was greatly relieved—until the next time he needed money. In response to his request for another loan, the creditor handed him fake coins.

We sound the *shofar* for thirty days—the entire month of Elul—as a reminder to produce the spiritual money—good deeds—we require on Rosh Hashanah and Yom Kippur.

If we fail to procure properly minted coins, and instead declare as the Egyptians did before Joseph: *Ki tam hakesef el adoni* (Genesis 47:18), *The money* [kesef] *to my master has been finished,* implying that we experience no *kosef,* yearning, for our Master, lacking motivation for *mitzvot,* then we have only our blemished coins to offer G-d on Yom Kippur.

Conversely, if we heed the *shofar's* call, we will fulfill the deeper significance of the injunction, *You shall bind up the money in your hand, and you shall go to the place that the L-rd, your G-d, will choose* (Deuteronomy 14:25). In return, we can secure blessings of great abundance, as the verse continues, *You shall turn that money into whatever your soul desires—cattle, sheep, new wine, or old wine, or whatever your soul desires* (ibid., v. 26).

A Delay That Inspires Two Returns

וְזֶהוּ "כִּי לוּלֵא הִתְמַהְמָהְנוּ". 'לוּלֵא' אוֹתִיּוֹת 'אֱלוּל', "לוּלֵא
הִתְמַהְמָהְנוּ", כִּי הָאָדָם מִתְמַהְמֵהַּ וּמַאֲרִיךְ בְּחֶשְׁבּוֹן נַפְשׁוֹ
בְּחֹדֶשׁ אֱלוּל הִנֵּה אָז שַׁבְנוּ פַּעֲמָיִם, כְּלוֹמַר לְפִי אֹפֶן זֶה תִּהְיֶה
הָעֲבוֹדָה בִּשְׁנֵי אוֹפַנֵּי הַתְּשׁוּבָה דְּראשׁ הַשָּׁנָה וְיוֹם הַכִּפּוּרִים.

For had we not tarried, we would have returned twice by now
(Genesis 43:10).

This verse alludes to our spiritual goals for the months of
Elul and Tishrei:

Returning twice implies two forms of *teshuvah*—returning
to G-d. The first is an overall return experienced during Rosh
Hashanah, when we accept G-d as our King. The second, more
detailed return is that of Yom Kippur, when we cleanse and
purify ourselves from specific sins.

These two returns require prior self-reckoning during the
month of Elul. In the above phrase, *Had we not tarried*, the word

lulei (had we not) contains the same letters as Elul. If we tarry appropriately during Elul, taking the time to improve ourselves, then we can successfully return twice—on Rosh Hashanah and again on Yom Kippur.

In addition to the more generalized preparations during Elul, we require specific periods of preparation for each of our two subsequent returns. The first of these is the days of *Selichot* at the end of Elul, prior to Rosh Hashanah. We plead for mercy and offer heartfelt supplications like a servant pleading for his master's mercy, driven by our understanding that *To You, G-d, is the righteousness, and to us, shamefacedness...* (Daniel 9:7, *Selichot* prayers). The second period is the Days of Repentance between Rosh Hashanah and Yom Kippur, when we make a highly specific self-accounting before our second return—the *teshuvah* of Yom Kippur.

FOCUS

Self-improvement is not instant; plan your path of return.

Tears of Joy

הֲלֹא רֹאשׁ הַשָּׁנָה הוּא יוֹם טוֹב, וּבַמִּשְׁנָה 'יוֹם טוֹב שֶׁל רֹאשׁ הַשָּׁנָה',
וְהוּא יוֹם שִׂמְחָה, עַל כֵּן אוֹמְרִים שֶׁהֶחֱיָנוּ. וּמַה שֶּׁכָּתַב הָאֲרִיזַ"ל לִבְכּוֹת,
הוּא עֲבוּר גָּלוּת שְׁכִינָה וכו', וּכְדֵי שֶׁיִּדוּנֵנוּ הַשֵּׁם יִתְבָּרֵךְ לְטוֹבָה.
וְהוּא שֶׁכָּתוּב "לְכוּ אִכְלוּ מַשְׁמַנִּים וגו' וְאַל תֵּעָצֵבוּ כִּי חֶדְוַת ה' הִיא
מָעֻזְּכֶם", וְהַבְּכִיָּה שֶׁבּוֹכִין הוּא בְּכִיָּה שֶׁל שִׂמְחָה עַל שֶׁהֶחֱיָנוּ וְהִגִּיעָנוּ.

The Sages teach: "Even if a sharp sword rests on your neck,
do not prevent yourself from praying for mercy." This teaching
has been applied to Rosh Hashanah: A sharp sword of judgment
rests upon the necks of the Jewish people, and our souls sense
it. Nevertheless, we do not despair of G-d's mercy, and we weep
before Him with a full heart.

This view of Rosh Hashanah is troubling, because isn't it a
Yom Tov? In the Mishnah, our Sages refer to is it *Yom Tov shel
Rosh Hashanah,* the festival of Rosh Hashanah. It is a day of
joy! We even recite *Shehecheyanu,* thanking G-d for bringing
us to this *joyous* occasion. Indeed, it is stated regarding Rosh
Hashanah, *Go, eat rich foods and drink sweet drinks...and do not*

be sad, for the joy of G-d is your strength (Nechemiah 8:10). We weep tears of *joy* for having merited this auspicious occasion.

At the same time, precisely because it is a day of joy, we must recall Jerusalem—*If I do not recall Jerusalem at the head of my joy* (Psalms 137:6).[1] This we accepted to do with a vow and also a curse—*If I forget you, Jerusalem…* (ibid., v. 5). Therefore, when the Arizal mentions weeping on Rosh Hashanah, he refers to weeping over the exile and concealment of the Divine Presence. The great merit of our concern with the state of the *Shechinah* brings us favorable judgment.

FOCUS

Rather than praying to G-d, pray for G-d this Rosh Hashanah.

---

1. Note the association of *the head* [rosh] *of my joy* and Rosh Hashanah, the "head of the year."

Shofar in Heaven

זֶה סֵדֶר הַתְּקִיעוֹת תְּקִיעָה שְׁבָרִים תְּרוּעָה: דִּתְקִיעָה דָּא אַבְרָהָם,
שְׁבָרִים דָּא יִצְחָק, תְּרוּעָה דָּא יַעֲקֹב, וְכַאֲשֶׁר הָאָדָם צוֹעֵק 'אַבָּא
וּמַלְכִּי הַצִּילֵנִי וְרַחֲמֵנִי' הִנֵּה נוֹתֵן כֹּחַ בְּמִדַּת הָרַחֲמִים לְהִתְגַּבֵּר.

How is the *shofar* sounded in heaven on Rosh Hashanah?
First, the Almighty—the Great and Awesome G-d—seats
Himself upon the sublime throne, seat of Divine judgment.

Then our father Abraham, motivated by immense love,
pleads before G-d, begging Him to rise from the throne of
judgment and to ascend the throne of mercy. As the *Zohar*
states, "Abraham establishes the throne"—he requests that G-d
ascend the throne of mercy.

Isaac then arouses himself tremendously, reminding G-d of
the *akeidah* (Binding of Isaac) and pleading for his descendants.
As a result of his tremendous efforts, all obstacles and blockages
caused by our sins are cast aside.

Jacob then awakens abundant mercies upon us, our teacher Moses stands in supplication, the shepherds of our people stand at his side and exert themselves greatly in prayer, and supernal angels and good advocates usher in the merits of the Jewish people. Opposing them are the angels who level accusations.

Every thought, deed, and action—good or otherwise—of each Jew is then carefully reviewed, while the patriarchs and Moses advocate for the good of each Jew in turn.

This explains the order of the *shofar*'s sounds: a *tekiah* followed by *shevarim* and *teru'ah*. The *tekiah* is Abraham. The *shevarim* is Isaac. The *teru'ah* is Jacob.

When we use the occasion to cry out, "Father! My King! Save me! Have mercy on me!" we supply the supernal attribute of mercy with the power to overcome the prosecution.

FOCUS

As the *shofar* is blown, G-d's mercy is aroused, and our forefathers and the righteous are on your side. Accept G-d as King and ask Him to have pity on you.

Trained for War

הָעָם אֵינָם סוֹמְכִים עַל הַגִּבּוֹר רַק הֵם עַצְמָם יוֹדְעֵי תְּרוּעַת
הַמִּלְחָמָה, וְאָז "בְּאוֹר פָּנֶיךָ יְהַלֵּכוּן" לִקְרַאת הַמֶּלֶךְ.

There was once a country that relied on the incredible strength of a most mighty warrior for its defense. So mighty was he that none of his fellow citizens took pains to learn the art of warfare, because they relied on his strength alone for protection. Then came the fateful day of hostilities against a cunning enemy. The foes knew the folly of attempting to meet the mighty man head on, so instead they carried out covert operations to steal his weapons one at a time, until he found himself unarmed. Only then did they embark in open warfare, and they captured not only the unarmed warrior but the entire unarmed country as well.

Each year, immediately after sounding the *shofar* during the Rosh Hashanah service, we recite in unison: *Fortunate is the people that knows the shofar blast; G-d, they will walk in the light of Your countenance* (Psalms 89:16).

How fortunate are we that we are a nation whose individual members *know the shofar blast.* We have mighty spiritual giants among us, but instead of relying on them alone, each of us learns how to sound the battle cry for himself. For example, the *Tur* mentions a custom for the public to fast on the day preceding Rosh Hashanah—despite the fact that our greatest individuals pour forth their mightiest spiritual efforts on this day.

As a result of our individual efforts, we are guaranteed to *walk in the light of Your countenance,* to meet the King on Rosh Hashanah.

FOCUS

Our nation requires your input this Rosh Hashanah.

Come With Coins

'שָׁלַח לוֹ רַבָּן' — רַב שֶׁל כָּל הָעוֹלָמוֹת, 'גַּמְלִיאֵל' — הַגּוֹמֵל
חֶסֶד חֲסָדִים טוֹבִים, 'גּוֹזְרַנִי כו' שֶׁתָּבוֹא בְּמַקֶּלְךָ' — לְהַצִּיל
עַצְמְךָ מִיַּד הַשָּׂטָן וְהַמַּסְטִינִים הַחוֹחִים וְהַקּוֹצִים, לְקַדֵּם
בְּרוֹעִים וּבְמַקְּלוֹת, 'וּמְעוֹתֶיךָ' — שֶׁהֵם מַעֲשִׂים טוֹבִים.

Rabban Gamliel calibrated the calendar in a manner questionable to his colleagues. When R. Yehoshua announced his intention to follow a different calculation, Rabban Gamliel sent him a message: "I decree that you come to me with your cane and money on the day that according to your reckoning is Yom Kippur!"

Rabban, "master," alludes to the Master of the universe, Who is "Gamliel": *Gomel* means benevolent bestowal, as in *gemilas chessed*, bestowal of kindness, and *E-l* is the Divine name of *chessed*, kindness.

"Come...with your cane": A stick indicates actions necessary to rescue oneself from the accusatory forces. "Come with...your money" is an allusion to good deeds. These we acquire during Elul. We subsequently approach G-d to repay His benevolence with good currency—our positive efforts—and collect blessings of great abundance in return.

However, one who lacks genuine currency repays with blemished coins. The twenty-two letters of the Torah are "the King's currency." If they are blemished coins, they are a list of sins, as per the Yom Kippur confession (based on the twenty-two letters): "*Ashamnu*, we transgressed, *bagadnu*, we acted deceitfully, *gazalnu*, We robbed, etc." He offers G-d a payment of falsehood.

When he wishes to borrow further blessings for the coming year, he receives blemished currency, as per the liturgy: "*Ashamnu mikol am*, we are guiltier than all people, *boshnu mikol dor*, we are more shameful than all generations, *gallah mimenu massos*, joy has departed from us... Our Land's beauty went to foreigners, our strength to strangers... Many troubles encompassed us..." etc.

FOCUS

All the Master of Benevolence asks of you is sincere effort.

Infinite G-d

מַה שֶׁקּוֹרִין לְמָחֳרַת יוֹם הַכִּפּוּרִים "גָאטס נָאמֶען", הִנֵּה שֵׁם הַוָיָ'
וְשֵׁם קֻדְשָׁא בְּרִיךְ הוּא אֵינוֹ אֶלָּא מַה שֶׁשַּׁיָךְ לְעוֹלָם, אֲפִילוּ לְעוֹלָם
הַנֶּאֱצָלִים, אַךְ לְעַצְמוּתוֹ אֵינוֹ שַׁיָךְ לִקְרוֹתוֹ בְּשׁוּם שֵׁם שֶׁבָּעוֹלָם,
וְהִנֵּה אִם פּוֹגֵם הוּא בְּשֵׁם הַוָיָ' דַוְקָא וְכַיָדוּעַ, וּבִימֵי סְלִיחוֹת
הֶעָוֹן יֵשׁ עֲלִיּוֹת לִפְנֵי הַוָיָ', וְזֶה לְמָחֳרַת יוֹם הַכִּפּוּרִים אֵין לוֹ שׁוּם
שֵׁם פְּרָטִי — לֹא הַוָיָ' וְלֹא אֲדֹנָ־י — רַק "גָאטס נָאמֶען".

The sacredness of Yom Kippur does not disappear when the
fast is over. In fact, the day following Yom Kippur is customarily
referred to in Yiddish as *G-tt's Nomen*, the day of G-d's Name.

G-d has many names, such as *HaVaYah*, or *Kudsha Brich
Hu* ("The Holy One blessed be He"), and so on. However, they
all refer to dimensions of G-dliness that are associated with the
created worlds. A particular name might be associated with
the most sublime world of *atzilut,* but even *atzilut* is ultimately
referred to as a world, implying a limitation of sorts. Therefore,
all of G-d's names imply limitation, albeit subtly. By contrast,
G-d Himself—meaning His very Essence—infinitely transcends
creation to the point that it cannot be given a name or title
at all.

As is well known, a person who commits a sin inflicts a blemish upon the Divine name *HaVaYah*. During the Days of Forgiveness, his *teshuvah* causes an ascent to a dimension that the Torah describes as being *lifnei HaVaYah*, before G-d— transcending even the most sublime Divine name. The result of connecting with the Infinite is that the blemish inflicted upon the name *HaVaYah* is rectified. This is the superiority of the *teshuvah* achieved on Yom Kippur.

Reflecting this unique connection with the Infinite, the day immediately following Yom Kippur that is illuminated by the transcendent quality of Yom Kippur is referred to not by the name *HaVaYah* or any other specific Divine name, but simply as *G-tt's Nomen*, the undefined reference to G-d's Essence.

FOCUS

On Yom Kippur, you received power from G-d's Essence. Now put it to good use.

G-d's Loving Embrace

יוֹם הָרִאשׁוֹן דְּחַג הַסֻּכּוֹת הוּא 'רִאשׁוֹן לְחֶשְׁבּוֹן עֲווֹנוֹת', כְּמַאֲמַר
רַזַ"ל עַל פָּסוּק וּלְקַחְתֶּם לָכֶם בַּיּוֹם הָרִאשׁוֹן, וּמְשַׁל הַחִבּוּק זֶה
עִנְיַן וִימִינוֹ תְּחַבְּקֵנִי דְּחַג הַסֻּכּוֹת — הַקָּפַת הַסְּכַךְ דְּסֻכָּה כו'.

A king sent his precious son to other kingdoms to acquire wisdom and experience. The prince traveled far, squandering his wealth on newly discovered pleasurable excesses. He wound up lonely and penniless in a region so distant that nobody had heard of his father.

Struggling for survival, he longed for home. The journey home was arduous, but when the king saw his long-lost son returning in genuine remorse, he forgave the prince for his errant choices and embraced him with passionate love.

We are G-d's children. He sends our souls on distant journeys into corporeal bodies to study Torah and perform *mitzvot* so we can earn an unprecedented ascent. We grow corrupted through love for our bodies, money, and human cravings. Our immersion in pleasures leaves our souls terribly distanced from G-d—where He is not recognized. Our souls forget their former spirituality, becoming impoverished spiritually and materially, a condition aggravated by our protracted exile.

When a Jew suddenly returns to G-d, as we do during Tishrei, G-d's mercy erupts at the sight of His lost beloved son. G-d absolves our waywardness on Yom Kippur, and He warmly embraces us during Sukkot. As our Sages state on the verse, *Take [the lulav] for yourselves on the first day…* (Leviticus 23:40): "This is *'the first day'* for reckoning sins," because our record was cleansed on Yom Kippur. G-d embraces us, enveloping us with the *sukkah* walls and the *sechach*, as it is stated, *His right arm embraced me* (Song of Songs 2:6).

Torn Shoes in Paradise

אוּן דֶער מִיט הָאט זִיךְ מַלְאָךְ מִיכָאֵל מִתְגָּאֶה גִיוֶוען אוֹיפֿ׳ן
מַלְאָךְ מְטַ״ט, וָואס עֶר אִיז קוֹשֶׁר כְּתָרִים לְקוֹנוֹ מִתְּפִלוֹתֵיהֶן שֶׁל
יִשְׂרָאֵל, אוּן עֶר — מַלְאָךְ מִיכָאֵל — וֶועט מַאכְן אַ בֶּעסֶערְן
כֶּתֶר פֿוּן דִי שִׂמְחַת תּוֹרָה טֶענְץ צֶערִיסֶענֶע פַֿאנטָאפֶֿעל.

Shacharit is scheduled later on Shabbat and Yom Yov than during the week, but on the morning of Simchat Torah in particular, people involuntarily sleep in after the exertion of the night's *hakafot*, followed by a festive Yom Tov meal.

Angels do not have *hakafot* and Yom Tov meals. They begin their day as usual, desiring to sing praises to their Creator. They cannot do so without the participation of the Jewish souls on earth, as our Sages derive from the verse, *When the morning stars sing together* (Job 38:7): "The ministering angels do not sing G-d's praises Above until the Jews sing His praises below." But today, the Jews are late.

The angels spend the hiatus tidying the Garden of Eden. They discover unfamiliar objects: shoes, slippers, heels. They are utterly mystified. They are used to *tzitzit, tefillin,* and other objects used for *mitzvot,* but not shoes!

They consult the archangel Michael. He replies, "These are *my* merchandise!" He explains that these items come from the Jews' exuberant dancing with the Torah and begins sorting them, "These shoes are from the Jews of Kaminka, these are from the Jews of Mezritch...."

With these broken shoes, Michael gloats over the archangel Matat, "Your duty is to tie crowns for our Creator from the Jewish prayers, but I will fashion a far superior crown from the lost shoes and torn heels of their Simchat Torah dancing!"

FOCUS

Dance with the Torah until your heels loosen and the night expires, because tonight you are G-d's crown.

Let There Be Light

וְזֶהוּ שֶׁכָּתוּב 'וְאֵינִי יוֹדֵעַ בְּאֵיזֶה מֵהֶם חָפֵץ', מֵאַחַר שֶׁגַּם מַעֲשֵׂה
הָרְשָׁעִים הוּא כְּסֵא לְמַעֲשֵׂה הַצַּדִּיקִים, אִם כֵּן הַכֹּל אַחְדוּת אֶחָד.
לְכָךְ נֶאֱמַר "וַיַּרְא אֱלֹהִים אֶת הָאוֹר כִּי טוֹב' — אֵלּוּ מַעֲשֵׂיהֶם
שֶׁל צַדִּיקִים", כִּי בְּמַעֲשֵׂה הָרְשָׁעִים צָרִיךְ הַבְדָּלָה וכו'.

And it was evening and it was morning (Genesis 1:5).

The Midrash explains: "*And it was evening*—this refers to
the deeds of the wicked. *And it was morning*—this refers to the
deeds of the righteous. We do not know which of these G-d
desires. The Torah therefore continues, *And G-d saw the light that
it was good* (Genesis 1:3), indicating that He desires the deeds of
the righteous."

This teaching is bewildering: Why might we assume that
G-d prefers evil deeds over righteous acts?

The answer is that there is *the advantage of light from
darkness* (Ecclesiastes 2:13), meaning that the superiority of light
is recognizable only in the presence of darkness, which creates

a contrast. Similarly, a wise man's superiority is amplified by the presence of a fool, and a *tzaddik's* superiority is clarified by the presence of a wicked person.

We can now appreciate the Midrash's statement: "We do not know which of these G-d desires." Abhorrent actions serve as a throne upon which deeds of righteousness rise, clarifying the beauty and sanctity of leading a righteous life. We might therefore consider positive and wicked deeds as belonging to a single global scheme, and, subsequently, earning equal significance in G-d's eyes.

The Torah dispels this notion with its emphatic statement that *G-d saw the light that it was good*—"this refers to the deeds of the righteous." True, the actions of the wicked ultimately serve a purpose, but we must unequivocally distinguish them from positive deeds and reject them as undesirable.

FOCUS

Provide your sacred ends
with sacred means.

PURIM I

Maiden Voyage

"וּבְהַגִּיעַ תֹּר נַעֲרָה וְנַעֲרָה לָבוֹא כו'", שֶׁהוּא הַנִּיצוֹץ הַנְּתוּנָה
בְּעָמְקֵי הַקְּלִפּוֹת [הַנִּקְרָא נַעֲרָה] שֶׁמְנוּעֶרֶת מִכָּל טוּב וְרוֹצָה
לְהִתְדַּבֵּק בְּשָׁרְשָׁהּ, וְהִגִּיעַ עֵת וּזְמַן לְהַעֲלוֹתָהּ בִּקְדֻשָׁה, הִנֵּה אָז
צָרִיךְ לְהִתְעוֹרֵר [מְאֹד] מְאֹד, כִּי לֹא לְחִנָּם בָּאָה [זֹאת] הַמַּחֲשָׁבָה
אֶלָּא לְהַעֲלוֹתָהּ, וְאִם לֹא עַכְשָׁו אֵימָתַי, אֶפְשָׁר לֹא יִהְיֶה עוֹד עֵת
וְתֹר הַנַּעֲרָה הַהִיא, כִּי עַל פִּי רֹב הַמַּחֲשָׁבָה בָּאָה מֵעִנְיָן הַדוֹמֶה
לְעִנְיַן הַתְּפִלָּה וְהַבְּרָכָה הַהִיא [אוֹ מֵעִנְיַן הַלִּמּוּד שֶׁהוּא עוֹסֵק].

As each maiden's turn arrived to go to the king (Esther 2:12).

While praying or studying, we might find ourselves interrupted by distracting thoughts. These are not random; the thoughts are the maidens that arrive precisely at their appropriate time, in the sincere desire to go to the King.

Here's a parable: A father asks someone to test his son on Jewish law. The examiner poses difficult questions and attempts to confuse the son and distort his comprehension of the material. The father does not want his son to be confused and left with mistaken conclusions. He wants his son to concentrate and solve the difficult questions, avoid the pitfalls, and prove his worth as an expert student. The son's triumph will bring the father tremendous joy, in the spirit of the verse, *Be wise, my son; cause my heart to rejoice, that I may answer him who taunts me* (Proverbs 27:11).

Similarly, alien thoughts arrive not for the sake of undermining prayer or study but for a positive purpose:

The word *na'arah* (נערה), maiden, refers to an entity that is *menu'aret* (מנוערת), excluded—meaning the sparks of holiness that are entirely trapped within the forces of evil and are thereby excluded from all goodness. They long to be reattached to their original source in holiness—to come to the King.

They seize their chance when a person studies or prays, each spark arriving at its appropriate time. For our mind wanders from the topic on which we are concentrating to a related albeit corrupted topic that presents as a distracting or improper thought. The "maiden," the spark trapped in a particular strain of improper thought, is related to the precise theme of our study or prayer.

We must respond with redoubled concentration, because our additional efforts will allow the entrapped spark to find the reattachment to its source that it so desperately seeks.

FOCUS

What you consider an obstacle might be something begging for redemption.

Purim of the Present

'הַקּוֹרֵא אֶת הַמְגִלָּה לְמַפְרֵעַ לֹא יָצָא', וְוֶן אֵיינֶער לֵייעֶנְט דִי
מְגִלָּה אוּן עֶר מֵיינְט אַז דֶער סִיפּוּר וָואס וֶוערְט דָּארְט דֶערְצֵיילְט
הָאט פַּאסִירְט (נָאר) אַמָאל, לְמַפְרֵעַ, אוּן נִיט אִיצְטֶער אִיז
דֶער נֶם, אִיז, אִיז — לֹא יָצָא. דֶער תַּכְלִית פוּן קְרִיאַת הַמְגִלָּה אִיז
אָפְּצוּלֶערְנֶען זִיךְ פוּן אִיר וִוי אַ אִיד דַארְף זִיךְ פִירְן אִיצְטֶער.

The Sages teach: *"One who reads the Megillah out of sequence
has not fulfilled his obligation."*

The term *l'mafrei'a*, out of sequence, literally means
retroactively or after the fact—indeed, that is its usual definition
in matters of Jewish law.

We can apply this understanding of the term to the above
teaching as well to provide us with a deeper message:

If we read the Megillah as if it were after the fact—as the
narrative of a historic event that occurred *l'mafrei'a*, long ago,
then we have not fulfilled our obligation. Rather, we must read

it as a present and ongoing occurrence, because the purpose of reading the Megillah is to discover the ways in which we are meant to conduct ourselves at present.

FOCUS

Listen carefully; the Megillah is speaking to your situation.

National Repair

"וְקַבֵּל הַיְּהוּדִים" — מִיט מְסִירוּת־נֶפֶשׁ'דִיגָן קַבָּלַת־עוֹל הָאבָּן זֵיי
מְתַקֵּן גֶעוֶוען "אֶת אֲשֶׁר הֵחֵלּוּ", אָט דָאס וָואס זֵיי הָאבָּן וָואכֲעדִיג
גֶעמַאכְט, מְצַד זֵייעֶר וָואכֲעדִיגְקֵייט וָואס קוּמְט פוּן חוֹלַאת רוּחְנִי.

The Jews accepted upon themselves that which they had commenced to do (Esther 9:23).

What did they accept upon themselves? To serve G-d with *kabbalat ol*, absolute acceptance of the yoke of heaven. Under threat of Haman's decree, they demonstrated *kabbalat ol* with pure self-sacrifice. They thereby rectified *that which they had commenced to do*. The word *heicheilu*, commenced, is related to *chol*, mundane, and *cholah*, illness. They rectified all that they had previously made mundane—profaned—as a result of their spiritual sicknesses. Focusing solely on G-d's will provided an instant cure, and thereby an instant rectification.

FOCUS

Purim empowers you to repair your past through your present.

Freedom of the Firstborn

בְּכוֹר נִקְרָא דָּבָר חִידּוּשׁ, הַנֶּאֱמַר בְּרֹאשׁ, וְהוּא דָּבָר שֵׂכֶל וּמַשְׂכִּיל שֶׁיַּשְׂכִּיל בְּשִׂכְלוֹ הַקּוֹדֶשׁ אֵיךְ לִנְהוֹג בַּעֲבוֹדַת הַשֵּׁם יִתְבָּרֵךְ.

Why did G-d orchestrate the exodus from Egypt in such a manner so that the blow to the Egyptians that immediately freed the Jewish people was the death of the firstborns?

The intellect is the firstborn within us, the first of our faculties. Its role is to serve as a guide for our service to G-d, directing us in the appropriate steps. There is, however, a rival firstborn that is supplied by the forces of evil. Its goal is to disrupt the intellect's attachment to G-d and to drive a wedge between us and G-d.

The result of the evil firstborn's presence is the Egyptian Exile, the spiritual constraints caused by not focusing properly on G-d and not allowing our spiritual realizations to flow into actual Divine service.

The death of the evil firstborn and the rejection of the forces of evil leads to an automatic and immediate liberation from the exile of our intellectual potentials.

FOCUS

Your bond with G-d begins with forcing yourself to focus.

A Personalized
Approach

אױפֿן פּסוק ״וַיֵּרֶד הֲוֵי׳ עַל הַר סִינַי״ זָאגְט דֶער תַּרְגּום ״וְאִתְגְּלִי
ה׳ עַל טוּרָא דְסִינַי״... װָאס דִי כַּוָנָה אִיז הִתְגַּלוּת, װָאס הִתְגַּלוּת
מֵיינְט אַ גִילוּי וֶועלְכֶער קֶען צוּגֶענוּמֶען וֶוערֶן אױך אֲפִילוּ אִין
דִי גָאר נִידֶעריגְסְטֶע דַרְגוֹת, װִי אִין מַתַּן תּוֹרָה אִיז גֶעווֶען אַז
אַלֶע, פֿון דֶער הֶעכְסְטֶער דַרְגָא װִי מֹשֶׁה רַבֵּינוּ בִּיז דֶעם פָּחוּת
שֶׁבְּיִשְׂרָאֵל, הָאבְּן מְקַבֵּל גֶעווֶען פֿון מַתַּן תּוֹרָה, אוּן דָאס מֵיינְט דֶער
תַּרְגּום וְאִתְגְּלִי מַלְאֲכָא דַה׳ אַז דָאס אִיז אַ עִנְיָן פֿון הִתְגַּלוּת.

And G-d descended upon Mount Sinai (Exodus 19:20).

The word *vayeired, And He descended*, appears in numerous other verses. On each occasion, *Targum Onkelos* translates it into the equivalent phrase in Aramaic. The one exception is in the above verse that introduces G-d's giving of the Torah at Sinai. In this case, *Targum Onkelos* uses the Aramaic *itgelli*, meaning, He revealed Himself, from the Hebrew *hitgalut*, self-revelation.

In truth, *hitgalut* also implies a descent of sorts, because it connotes a revelation that is so powerful that it reaches down to the spiritually lowest and furthest regions of existence. That is precisely what occurred at the Giving of the Torah; the revelation was of such a nature that allowed every Jew—from Moses, the ultimate prophet, down to the lowliest member of our people—to effectively receive the G-dly revelation.

FOCUS

On Shavuot, G-d descends to your level and says, "Please accept My Torah."

A Clean Palace

כְּשֶׁהָאָדָם מְחַשֵׁב בִּדְבֵקוּת הַשֵׁם יִתְבָּרֵךְ בָּרוּךְ הוּא אֲזַי [מִיָּד] שׁוֹרֶה עִמּוֹ
וְשׁוֹכֵן אֶצְלוֹ. בְּכֵן רָאוּי לְאָדָם שֶׁיִּתְרַחֵק עַצְמוֹ מִן הַתַּאֲוֹות וּמַחֲשָׁבוֹת
זָרוֹת בִּכְדֵי שֶׁלֹּא יִפָּרֵד מִמֶּנּוּ יִתְבָּרֵךְ, רַק יַעֲשֶׂה כָּל מַעֲשָׂיו לִשְׁמוֹ יִתְבָּרֵךְ.
וְזֶהוּ 'הַרְחֵק מִשָׁכֵן רָע', רוֹצֶה לוֹמַר מִפִּי שֶׁשׁוֹכֵן אֶצְלְךָ הַרְחֵק הָרָע.

"Keep distant from an evil neighbor" (Avot 1:7).

The term *shachein*, neighbor, comes from the word meaning to dwell. We can therefore offer an alternative reading of the above teaching. Instead of *harcheik mishachein ra*, keep distant from an evil neighbor, it can be understood as if were written, *harcheik ra mishachein*, keep evil distant from he who dwells.

What does this mean?

It says, *Seek G-d when He is found, call Him when He is near* (Isaiah 55:6), implying that G-d is restricted at times. By contrast, *From there you will seek G-d...you will find Him if you seek Him* (Deuteronomy 4:29) implies that G-d is available at all times. Similarly, *For what great nation is there that has G-d so near to it, as the L-rd, our G-d, is at all times that we call upon Him?* (ibid., v. 7).

The first verse addresses the era of the Holy Temple, when great effort was required to approach G-d and receive Divine inspiration. During exile, it is far easier to receive answers to prayers and to merit Divine inspiration.

Here is a parable: A person cannot approach a king in his palace at random and for any purpose. When a king tours the country, however, even a peasant who would not be received at the palace can encounter the king and share a concern.

During exile, whenever we focus on G-d, He dwells within us. "Keep evil distant from He Who dwells [within you]." We must distance ourselves from corporeal desires and unholy thoughts, so that G-d will not depart.

FOCUS

Sacred words and deeds are not enough; you must also keep the place clean.

Torah for the Jews

מוֹרֵנוּ הַבַּעַל שֵׁם טוֹב הָאט גֶעזָאגְט אוֹיף דֶעם מַאֲמָר 'כָּל תּוֹרָה
שֶׁאֵין עִמָּהּ מְלָאכָה סוֹפָהּ בְּטֵלָה', מְלָאכָה מֵיינְט הִתְעַסְקוּת, 'כָּל
תּוֹרָה שֶׁאֵין עִמָּהּ מְלָאכָה', הִתְעַסְקוּת אֵין אַהֲבַת יִשְׂרָאֵל, 'סוֹפָהּ
בְּטֵלָה', יֶעדֶע שְׁטִיקֶעל תּוֹרָה וָואס מֶען לֶערְנְט אוּן עֶס בְּרֶיינְגְט נִיט
מְלָאכָה דָאס הֵייסְט אַהֲבַת יִשְׂרָאֵל, אִיז דִי תּוֹרָה קֵיין תּוֹרָה נִיט.

"All Torah study that is not accompanied with work is destined to be nullified" (*Avot* 2:2).

The term *melachah*, work, refers to an activity with which we are fully occupied. What occupation, or, better said, preoccupation, must accompany our Torah study? *Ahavat Yisrael*—love for a fellow Jew.

The Mishnah warns us that all Torah study that lacks this degree of *ahavat Yisrael* will be nullified, because any branch of Torah knowledge that does not bring us to *ahavat Yisrael* is not Torah.

FOCUS

Ask yourself while studying: How will this wisdom benefit someone?

Studying Solo

❧

'הַמְהַלֵּךְ בַּדֶּרֶךְ יְחִידִי וְשׁוֹנֶה וּמַפְסִיק מִמִּשְׁנָתוֹ כו''... הַהוֹלֵךְ בְּדֶרֶךְ
הַיָּשָׁר, וַאֲפִילוּ הָכִי הוּא יְחִידִי שֶׁאֵינוֹ דָבוּק בְּהַשֵּׁם יִתְבָּרֵךְ, 'וְשׁוֹנֶה וּמַפְסִיק
מִמִּשְׁנָתוֹ', רוֹצֶה לוֹמַר: מַפְסִיק אֶת עַצְמוֹ מֵהַשֵּׁם יִתְבָּרֵךְ מֵחֲמַת מִשְׁנָתוֹ,
דְּהַיְנוּ שֶׁבָּאָה לוֹ גַּדְלוּת וְהִתְפָּאֲרוּת מֵחֲמַת מִשְׁנָתוֹ שֶׁסּוֹבֵר שֶׁהוּא
מִשְׁנָתוֹ שֶׁלּוֹ... פֵּירוּשׁ: אֲפִילוּ כְּשֶׁמִּתְעַסֵּק בַּתּוֹרָה שֶׁנֶּאֱמַר בָּהּ "תּוֹרַת
ה' תְּמִימָה". וְזֶהוּ שֶׁכָּתוּב "תָּמִים תִּהְיֶה", אֲפִילוּ בְּעֵסֶק הַתּוֹרָה "תִּהְיֶה
עִם ה' אֱלֹקֶיךָ", וְלֹא תֵימָא הֲלֹא הַתּוֹרָה מִמֵּילָא נִקְרָא תּוֹרַת ה'.

❧

"One who … travels alone on the road and turns his heart to idleness has forfeited his life" (*Avot* 3:4).

"One who walks along a road and studies, and interrupts his studies to say, 'How beautiful is this tree!' or 'How beautiful is this ploughed field!'—the Torah considers it as if he had forfeited his life" (ibid. 3:7).

From a deeper perspective, these teachings describe a person who follows the path of Torah and *mitzvot*. However, he walks alone, without G-d, because he fails to attach himself to G-d.

"[He] studies, but he *interrupts* his studies." The interruption is not in his learning, but in his bond with G-d. The interruption is caused because it is "*his* studies," studies that are motivated by a desire for prestige, because he considers it "*his* studies," his own knowledge, for which he deserves credit.

"How beautiful is this tree!" He refers to himself, borrowing the metaphor: *Man is a tree of the field* (Deuteronomy 20:19). He considers himself great and powerful: *The tree grew and became strong; its height reached the sky, and its appearance was seen to the end of all the earth*" (Daniel 4:8).

"How beautiful is this ploughed field!" He refers to his portion in heaven, considering himself worthy of rewards.

"The Torah considers it as if he had forfeited his life." The Mishnah offers no supporting verse, because the *entire* Torah rejects his attitude. If you need a verse, here it is: *You shall be wholesome with G-d* (Deuteronomy 18:13). The Torah is called wholesome, so *You shall be wholesome* means that we must study Torah *with G-d*, while remaining firmly attached to G-d.

FOCUS

The Torah is G-d's; study it with humility.

Repel or Redirect

'אֵיזֶהוּ גִבּוֹר? הַכּוֹבֵשׁ אֶת יִצְרוֹ', קָשֶׁה דַּהֲוָה לֵיהּ לְמֵימַר מִי הוּא גִבּוֹר?
יֵשׁ לוֹמַר כְּמוֹ בְּעִסְקֵי הָעוֹלָם הַשּׁוֹמֵר לִשְׁמוֹר סְחוֹרָה וְשׁוֹמֵעַ גַּנָּב
חוֹתֵר, יֵשׁ צוֹעֵק וְעַל יְדֵי זֶה בּוֹרֵחַ הַגַּנָּב, וְיֵשׁ מֵכִין שַׁלְשְׁלָאוֹת וּכְשֶׁבָּא
הַגַּנָּב לַחֶדֶר הוּא אוֹסְרוֹ בְּכַבְלֵי בַרְזֶל. וְכֵן בְּצַדִּיקִים יֵשׁ אֵינוֹ מַנִּיחַ לִקְרַב
אֶצְלוֹ שׁוּם הִרְהוּר, וְכְדַרַב עַמְרָם חֲסִידָא, וְיֵשׁ לוֹקֵחַ הַחֶמְדָּה אוֹ אַהֲבָה
וְיִרְאָה רָעָה לַעֲבוֹדַת ה' לְאַהֲבָה וּלְיִרְאָה אוֹתוֹ יִתְבָּרֵךְ. וְזֶהוּ שֶׁכָּתוּב 'אֵיזֶהוּ
גִבּוֹר' יוֹתֵר, 'הַכּוֹבֵשׁ אֶת יִצְרוֹ' וּמִדּוֹתָיו וְחֶמְדָתוֹ לַעֲבוֹדַת הַשֵּׁם יִתְבָּרֵךְ.

"Who is strong? He who conquers his inclination. As it says (Proverbs 16:32), *He who is slow to anger is better than a strong man; he who rules his spirit is better than the captor of a city*" (Avot 4:1).

The wording is not *mi gibor*, who is strong? but *eizehu gibor*, which is strong? There are two candidates—which is *truly* mighty? But first, a parable:

A guard heard a burglar attempting to gain entry and raised the alarm. Hearing the commotion, the burglar fled. A second guard facing the same scenario kept silent, caught the thief red-handed, and tied him securely.

The same is true of *tzaddikim*: Some undermine the inclination's approach; a negative thought cannot intrude without his raising the alarm and frightening it away. Other *tzaddikim* keep silent, allowing the inclination to enter and make suggestions. They reply, "Before I go ahead, I will first apply the same desire to something sacred, such as Torah study." With their redoubled energy in a sacred endeavor, they utterly conquer the *yetzer hara*.

"He who is slow to anger is better than a strong man." A strong *tzaddik* denies entry, but the "slow to anger" (erech apayim) is patient (*erech*) with his *af* ("fury")—a name for the *yetzer hara*. He allows it to remain so he can control it to better serve G-d. *"He who rules his spirit is better than the captor of a city."* The strong banish inhabitants from a city—he chases the inclination away—but the mightiest keep it within the city and use it for G-d.

Miserly Contribution

﷼

מִדָּה זוֹ 'לֹא יִתֵּן וְלֹא יִתְּנוּ אֲחֵרִים' אֵינוֹ מִנּוֹתְנֵי הַצְּדָקָה... וּבֵאֵר
פָּסוּק "חִשַּׁבְתִּי דְרָכָי וָאָשִׁיבָה רַגְלַי אֶל עֵדוֹתֶיךָ"... כִּי דָוִד
הַמֶּלֶךְ עָלָיו הַשָּׁלוֹם הָיָה בְּמַזָּל שֶׁלֹּא עָלוּ לוֹ מַחְשְׁבוֹתָיו בַּעֲבוֹדַת
הַשֵּׁם יִתְבָּרֵךְ כָּהוֹגֶן... לְכָךְ הָיָה חוֹשֵׁב בִּדְרָכָיו הַגַּשְׁמִי וּמִמֵּילָא
הָיָה בְּהֵיפֶךְ וְכוּ'. וְזֶהוּ שֶׁכָּתוּב "חִשַּׁבְתִּי דְרָכָי" וְאָז "וָאָשִׁיבָה
רַגְלַי", רוֹצֶה לוֹמַר: אָשִׁיבָה לְהַרְגִּיל בּוֹ אֶל עֵדוֹתֶיךָ, וְהָבֵן.

﷼

"There are four kinds of charity contributors: One who wants
to give but does not want others to give is begrudging of others.
One who wants only others to give begrudges himself. One who
wants he and others to give is a *chassid*. One who wants neither
he nor others to give is wicked" (*Avot* 5:13).

How can one who wants neither he nor others to give be
considered one of the "four kinds of charity *contributors*"?

*I considered my ways, and I returned my feet to Your
testimonies* (Psalms 119:59). What does this mean? The Midrash
teaches that "*it was evening* refers to wicked deeds; *it was
morning* refers to righteous deeds. Which does G-d prefer? *G-d
saw the light that it was good*—He prefers righteousness."

Why might we think G-d prefers evil deeds? Consider the case of King David: He was born under the influence of *mazal Shabtai* (the constellation associated with *binah*) and struggled to concentrate on Divine service. He would consider the contrast between his corporeality and spirituality, prompting him to reject the former and embrace the latter with tremendous enthusiasm.

I considered my *ways* of corporeality. *And I returned my* feet *to Your testimonies—regel*, foot, is related to *regilut*, his "regular" focus on Divine matters. Thus his corporeality was indispensable in generating greater concentration.

Similarly, all negative things are contrast enablers for the positive. Nevertheless, G-d desires good, because evil's contribution is tangential.

He who desires neither himself nor others to give charity is indeed a contributor. His contribution is his miserliness that creates a contrast with the generosity of actual donors, making their deeds shine.

FOCUS

Contribute light not contrast.

Forced Pleasure

מֵחֲמַת גּוֹדֶל הַתְלַהֲבוּת [לְבוֹ] לַתּוֹרָה וְלַעֲבוֹדַת הַשֵּׁם יִתְבָּרֵךְ
לְמַעַן שְׁמוֹ בְּאַהֲבָה, לֹא יַחְשׁוֹב אֵלָיו הַתַּעֲנוּג שֶׁל הָעוֹלָם הַזֶּה.

"Torah is acquired…through minimizing pleasure…"
(*Avot* 6:6).

The least of the conditions for bonding with G-d through Torah and *mitzvot* is to divest from corporeal pleasures. Rather, the intensity of our fiery passion for Torah and Divine service— for the sake of G-d alone, out of pure love—renders corporeal pleasures meaningless.

This is similar to a businessman netting a windfall; he is so delighted with his staggering gain that he does not sense the minor pleasure of enjoying food.

The Mishnah does not state "with minimal [*me'at*] pleasure," but, "through minimizing [*mi'ut*] pleasure." Even a *little* corporeal pleasure is too much, because it undermines our attachment to G-d. We must focus on increasing our delight in cleaving to

G-d to the point that corporeal pleasures are diminished beyond significance, like "a lamp in the daylight."

Our Sages discuss "pleasure that comes against one's will," regarding a specific scenario where benefiting from a forbidden substance is unavoidable and without intention to derive benefit. Even if it is possible to avoid the substance in that scenario, there is an opinion that considers it permissible to use if the person does not intend to derive benefit.

Our Mishnah, by contrast, addresses *permissible* pleasures—eating, drinking, etc. If we intend to enjoy them, we sacrifice our ability to truly cleave to G-d with love through Torah and Divine service.

FOCUS

One heart cannot handle two conflicting loves.

The Power of Chitat

"וַיְהִי חִתַּת אֱלֹקִים וְגוֹ'" — "חִתַּת" רָאשֵׁי תֵבוֹת 'חוּמָשׁ' 'תְּהִלִּים'
'תַּנְיָא', וְהַבָּקִי בְּאוֹתִיּוֹתֵיהֶם מְשַׁבֵּר כָּל הַהֶעְלֵמוֹת וְהַהֶסְתֵּרִים.

The verse says, *And the terror of G-d was [upon the cities]...* (Genesis 35:5). The Hebrew word for terror is **Chitat** (*chet, tof, tof*), which is an acronym for *Chumash, Tehillim, Tanya*. A person who is erudite in their letters eradicates all challenges and concealments.

Words That Annul Decrees

"וּתְהִי לְרָצוֹן תָּמִיד עֲבוֹדַת יִשְׂרָאֵל עַמֶּךָ." הַפֵּרוּשׁ: תָּמִיד 'עֲבוֹדַת
יִשְׂרָאֵל עַמֶּךָ' עוֹשֶׂה רָצוֹן לְהַחְלִישׁ אֶת הַגְּזֵרָה וּלְבַטְּלָהּ, ו'עֲבוֹדַת
יִשְׂרָאֵל' שֶׁהִיא עוֹמֶדֶת תָּמִיד לִפְנֵי הַשֵּׁם יִתְבָּרֵךְ לַעֲשׂוֹת רָצוֹן טוֹב
הֵם אוֹתִיּוֹת שֶׁבַּתּוֹרָה... אֲמִירַת אוֹתִיּוֹת שֶׁבַּתּוֹרָה וְסֵפֶר תְּהִלִּים.

During the *amidah*, we recite the words: "May the service of
Your people Israel always find favor."

The meaning of this prayer is that the service of the Jewish
people always creates favor that serves to weaken and annul any
heavenly decree against them.

Which service of the Jewish people remains constantly
before G-d, working continually to generate good favor on their
behalf? It is the words of the Torah. When Jewish people read
the words that are in the actual Torah, and when they read the
book of Psalms.

What Is Your Connection

דִי אֱמֶת'עֶ תְּמִימוּת'/דִיקֶע אֱמוּנָה וָואס אַ פָּשׁוּטֶ'ר אִיד
אוּן אַ פָּשׁוּטֶע אִידֶענֶע זָאגְן תְּהִלִים אִיז דָאס דִי גְרֶעסְטֶע
דַרְגָּא פוּן דְּבֵיקוּת, דִי נְשָׁמָה אִיז בַּא אַלֶעמֶען גְלַיךְ.

Through demonstrating true and sincere faith while reciting
Psalms, any Jewish man or woman can achieve the spiritual
heights of *dveikut* (cleaving to G-d). After all, every Jew possesses
a G-dly soul. Therefore, every person—from the simplest Jewish
man, woman, or child, to the greatest Torah scholar—is able to
pour the faith of his or her soul into the holy words of prayer,
and to connect deeply with the sacred words that he or she
utters, thereby arousing G-d's mercy and bringing salvation.

Become an Expert

לוּ יָדְעוּ כֹּחַ שֶׁיֵּשׁ בְּצֵרוּפֵי אוֹתִיּוֹת הַתּוֹרָה לֹא הָיָה אֶחָד
מִיִּשְׂרָאֵל שֶׁלֹּא הָיָה בָּקִי בְּחוּמָשׁ וּבִתְהִלִּים.

If people only knew the power concealed in the combinations of the letters of the Torah, every single Jew would strive to become an expert in the words of Torah and Psalms!

The Power of Psalms

"מִי יְמַלֵּל גְּבוּרוֹת ה' יַשְׁמִיעַ כָּל תְּהִלָּתוֹ", פֵּירוּשׁ: יְמַלֵּל יְשַׁבְּרֵם
וִיבַטְּלֵם כְּמוֹ מוֹלְלִין מְלִילוֹת, וְהַכַּוָּנָה שֶׁיְבַטֵּל גְּבוּרוֹת ה'
פֵּירוּשׁ דִּינִין, "יַשְׁמִיעַ כָּל תְּהִלָּתוֹ", הַיְנוּ שֶׁיֹּאמְרוּ תְּהִלִּים שֶׁכֻּלּוֹ
תְּהִלּוֹת ד', וְעַל יְדֵי זֶה יְבַטֵּל וִישַׁבֵּר הַדִּינִין הַבָּאִין עָלָיו.

Who can recount G-d's mighty deeds? [Who can] make heard
all His praise? (Psalms 106:2).

The word for recount can also mean to shatter. And the
word for mighty acts can also mean severities. Accordingly, we
can read the verse as, "Who can shatter G-d's severities?" What
can we do to remove Heaven's adverse decree against us? The
answer is supplied in the continuation of the verse, *Make heard*
all His praise [tehillato]. Through reciting Psalms (Tehillim),
which is entirely dedicated to G-d's praises, we can remove His
severities that have been applied against us.

Sources

Note: Sources are based on *Keter Shem Tov*, Kehot Edition, fourth ed.

Bereishit
Source: *Keter Shem Tov*, addendum, 6.
Bereishit can be read as *bet reishit*—
Rashi, Ramban Genesis 1:1.

Noach
Source: *Keter Shem Tov*, addendum, 10.

Lech Lecha
Source: *Keter Shem Tov*, 26-27.

Vayeira
Source: *Keter Shem Tov*, 245.
Some angels are permitted to sing praise
before G-d only once a week, or even
once every fifty years—*Chullin* 91b.
Others recite a verse from Psalms—
Siddur Ha'Arizal (Rashar), 70b.
How can you praise the King at a time of
fury!—From the *Kinot* recited on Tishah
B'Av.

Chayei Sarah
Source: *Keter Shem Tov*, addendum, 100.
There are three kinds of generosity:
financial, physical, and intellectual.
Our patriarch Abraham excelled in all
three—*Orchot Tzaddikim, Sha'ar* 17 ["The
Gate of Generosity"].

He used his wealth to provide food
and drink to all passersby... He
exerted himself physically, personally
serving food to those who entered his
abode—see Genesis ch. 18; *Midrash
Rabbah*, Genesis 43:7.
As stated in *Sefer Yetzirah* end of ch. 5.

Toldot
Source: *Keter Shem Tov*, addendum, 101;
Igrot Kodesh (Rayatz), vol. 5, p. 246.
Abraham's facial appearance was
replicated only in Isaac—Rashi Genesis
25:19.

Vayeitzei
Source: *Keter Shem Tov*, 145.
Know what is above you...—*Avot* 2:1.

Vayishlach
Source: *Keter Shem Tov*, 387 (1).
Heaven judges a person in each
chamber and drives him from the
chamber—*Zohar II* 245:b, *I* 234a.

Vayeishev
Source: *Keter Shem Tov*, 194.
The world was created via ten
utterances—*Avot* 5:1.

Mikeitz

Source: *Keter Shem Tov*, 62.

If we were to go around and seek, would we find anyone like him?—Genesis 41:38.

Vayigash

Source: *Keter Shem Tov*, 251 (1).

Vayechi

Source: *Keter Shem Tov*, 61 (1).

Tzaddikim are emissaries of the *Shechinah* (Divine Presence). Their role is to pray for the welfare of the *Shechinah*, which languishes in exile—*Zohar I* 242a. *Shechinah* is also referred to as Jacob—*Zohar I* 145b.

Shemot

Source: *Keter Shem Tov*, addendum, 14.

Va'eira

Source: *Keter Shem Tov*, 393.

Moses was exceedingly humble—Numbers 12:3.

Bo

Source: *Keter Shem Tov*, 13–14.

What is the spirit of G-d? It is the soul within you—*Midrash Rabbah*, Genesis 8:1; *Yalkut Shimoni*, Genesis 4; *Midrash Tehillim* 139:5.

Torah is compared to water—*Bava Kama* 17a; *Ta'anit* 7a.

Beshalach

Source: *Keter Shem Tov*, 109.

Yitro

Source: *Keter Shem Tov*, 47.

This verse informs us that the Holy One, Blessed be He, held the mountain over them like a barrel—*Shabbat* 88a.

Mishpatim

Source: *Keter Shem Tov*, addendum, 15.

That a kosher *mikveh* contains purifying

power is a *chok*—*Mishneh Torah*, end of *Mikvaot*.

A donkey feels chilly even in midsummer's heat—*Shabbat* 53a.

Terumah

Source: *Keter Shem Tov*, 172; addendum, 71.

Ever since the Holy Temple was destroyed, all that G-d has in His world is the four cubits of *halachah*—*Berachot* 8b. *HaLaCHaH*, is an acronym for *Hari'u Lashem Kol Ha'aretz*—*Likkutei Torah*, Psalms 100.

Tetzaveh

Source: *Keter Shem Tov*, addendum, 49.

Ki Tisa

Source: *Keter Shem Tov*, 141.

Jews are thieves—*Avodah Zarah* 70a.

Vayakheil

Source: *Keter Shem Tov*, 114.

Areas for ritual slaughter within the *azarah*—*Zevachim* 47a, 55a.

Pekudei

Source: *Keter Shem Tov*, 51 (2).

Myriads of angels waiting to raise our prayers through myriads of heavenly chambers—see *Zohar II* 244b, 260b.

Vayikra

Source: *Keter Shem Tov*, 393.

Tzav

Source: *Keter Shem Tov*, 293.

Whoever occupies himself with the study of *olah* [the laws of the burnt-offering] is considered having offered an actual *olah*—*Menachot* 110a.

Shemini

Source: *Keter Shem Tov*, 194.

Tazria

Source: *Keter Shem Tov,* 120.

Metzora

Keter Shem Tov, 363.

Who is wise? He who learns from each person—*Avot* 4:1.

Acharei

Keter Shem Tov, 96.

Four individuals entered the *pardeis*—*Chagigah* 14b.

Pardeis (פרדס) is used as a reference to the Torah, because it the acronym for the four rungs of Torah—*Tikunei Zohar Chadash* 107c.

Whoever studies Torah *lishmah* merits many things and the Torah's secrets are revealed to him...—*Avot* 6:1.

Kedoshim

Source: *Keter Shem Tov,* addendum, 17.

If one Jew hates another, even without acting upon it in speech or action, he transgresses a prohibition—Leviticus 19:17; *Sefer Hamitzvot,* Negative Commandment 302.

Obligation of *ahavat Yisrael*—Leviticus 19:18; *Sefer Hamitzvot,* Positive Commandment 206.

Emor

Keter Shem Tov, 97.

Behar

Keter Shem Tov, 31; addendum, 21.

Because it comes readily to Moses—*Berachot* 33b.

Bechukotai

Keter Shem Tov, 159.

Study or practical deeds are superior—*Kiddushin* 40b.

One who studies the subject of a burnt-offering is considered having offered an actual burnt-offering—*Menachot* 110a.

Bamidbar

Keter Shem Tov, 31.

A body is the soul's wife—*Tikunei Zohar* 21, 61a.

Re'u Ben, Shama, Lavah, Yodeh—Genesis 29:32-35.

Naso

Keter Shem Tov, 249.

Beha'alotecha

Keter Shem Tov, 238.

We were born on a summit—*Tanchuma, Beshalach* 14; *Yalkut Shimoni,* Psalms 860.

Shelach

Keter Shem Tov, 145.

Draw Divine light to all the worlds though our prayer and study—*Zohar I* 134b; 185a.

The angels are sustained from our efforts—*Zohar I* 18b; *II* 132a.

Excessive humility undermines all this—see *Gittin* 56a.

Cf. teaching for Re'eh.

Korach

Keter Shem Tov, 393.

Moses... as a Jewish king—*Zevachim* 102a; *Tanchuma, Beha'alotecha* 9.

Korah's brilliance and Divine inspiration—*Midrash Rabbah,* Numbers 18:8, with *Maharzu.*

Moses hesitated to become the leader as G-d commanded—Exodus 4:13.

Chukat

Keter Shem Tov, 393.

Red is symbolic of *kelipah*—see *Zohar II* 236b; *Midrash Aggadah,* beginning of Chukat.

The cow is slaughtered and then burned, etc.—*Mishneh Torah, Parah Adumah* 5:1; *Tanchuma, Chukat* 4:23; *Midrash Aggadah,* ibid.

Arrogance can bring purity to those who need spiritual cleansing—see II Chronicles 17:6; Sanhedrin 37a.

Arrogance...destructive to those who are advanced in the service of G-d—*Sotah* 5a; *Mishneh Torah, Dei'ot* 2:3.

We should not serve G-d for personal gain or considerations—*Avot* 1:3.

They must invite a measure of haughtiness, a self-serving motivation—*Pesachim* 50b.

Balak
Keter Shem Tov, addendum 44; *Igrot Kodesh (Rayatz),* vol. 5, p. 348.

Pinchas
Keter Shem Tov, 8, 37.
Ta'anit 22a.

Matot
Keter Shem Tov, addendum, 3.

Masei
Keter Shem Tov, addendum, 23.

Devarim
Keter Shem Tov, addendum, 25.

Va'etchanan
Keter Shem Tov, addendum, 30.

Eikev
Keter Shem Tov, 153.
Is fearing G-d a small accomplishment? – *Berachot* 33b.
You shall fear G-d (Deuteronomy 6:13), this includes reverence for Torah sages—*Bava Kama* 41b.
Even if he is utterly unlearned—see *Avot* 2:5.

Re'eh
Keter Shem Tov, 145.
The humility of R. Zechariah caused the [Temple's] destruction—*Gittin* 56a.
Cf. teaching for Shelach.

Shoftim
Keter Shem Tov, addendum, 14.
The Torah compares mortals to trees—see Deuteronomy 20:19.
A Torah scholar is a fruit-bearing tree—*Ta'anit* 7a.

Ki Teitzei
Keter Shem Tov, 10.
G-d is our Husband... We are His wife—*Midrash Rabbah,* Numbers 9:45.
Three methods for a man to take a woman as his wife—*Kiddushin* 2a.

Ki Tavo
Keter Shem Tov, addendum, 3.
Why is the earth called *aretz*? Because it desires to perform its Creator's will—*Midrash Rabbah,* Genesis 5:8.

Nitzavim
Keter Shem Tov, addendum, 14.
The house filled entirely with luminance—*Sotah* 12a.

Vayeilech
Keter Shem Tov, addendum, 32, 40.

Ha'azinu
Keter Shem Tov, 232.

V'zot Habrachah (Simchat Torah)
Keter Shem Tov, 13; addendum, 53.

Elul
Keter Shem Tov, 325.
You shall bind up the money in your hand, and you shall go to the place that the L-rd, your G-d, will choose (Deuteronomy

14:25)—note that this verse speaks of money exchanged for the produce of *ma'aser sheini* (second tithe). Such money must have *tzurah shel ma'aseh,* an actual form; it must be minted coins bearing an image, and not bullion or uncoined metal (*Bava Metzia* 54a). Similarly, the spiritual payment required for Yom Kippur must have "an actual form," practical action.
Cf. teaching for Yom Kippur.

Selichot
Keter Shem Tov, addendum, 13.

Rosh Hashanah
Keter Shem Tov, 420.

Even if a sharp sword rests on your neck, do not prevent yourself from praying for mercy—*Berachot* 10a.

The festival of Rosh Hashanah—*Rosh Hashanah* 29b. See also Mordechai, *Rosh Hashanah,* ch. 1, 708.

It is a day of joy—see *Yerushalmi, Rosh Hashanah* 1:3; *Tur, Orach Chaim* 597:1.

Arizal mentions weeping on Rosh Hashanah—*Pri Eitz Chaim,* Gate of Shofar, ch. 5.

Tekiat Shofar I
Keter Shem Tov, addendum, 106.
Abraham establishes the throne—*Zohar III* 99b.

Tekiat Shofar II
Keter Shem Tov, 133.
A custom for the public to fast on the day preceding Rosh Hashanah—*Tur, Orach Chaim* 581.

Yom Kippur
Keter Shem Tov, 325.
Rabban Gamliel calibrated the calendar in a manner questionable to his colleagues—*Rosh Hashanah* 25a.
A stick indicates actions necessary to rescue oneself from the accusatory forces—as per the requirement of a hired shepherd whose flock is menaced with a wild beast. He must "meet it head on with sticks" (*Bava Metzia* 93b). Similarly, the positive activities required to combat the accusations of the Satan (the "wild beast") are referred to as sticks.
Cf. teaching for Elul.

Day After Yom Kippur
Keter Shem Tov, addendum, 110.
Customarily referred to in Yiddish as *G-tt's Nomen,* the day of G-d's Name—see *Eshel Avraham, Orach Chaim* 624.
G-d Himself—meaning His very Essence—infinitely transcends creation to the point that it cannot be given a name or title at all—see *Zohar II* 42b; *III* 257b.

Sukkot
Keter Shem Tov, addendum, 108.
Our souls forget their former spiritually, becoming impoverished spiritually and materially—see *Kiddushin* 82b ("I performed evil deeds, and I ruined my livelihood").
This is "the first day" for reckoning sins—*Tanchuma, Emor* 22; *Yalkut Shimoni,* Leviticus 651.

Simchat Torah
Keter Shem Tov, addendum, 114.
The ministering angels do not sing G-d's praises Above until the Jews sing His praises below—*Chullin* 91a.
Your duty is to tie crowns for our Creator from the Jewish prayers—*Zohar III* 37b.

Chanukah

Keter Shem Tov, 188.

And it was evening—this refers to
the deeds of the wicked. *And it was
morning*—this refers to the deeds of the
righteous—*Midrash Rabbah*, Genesis 2:5.
Cf. teaching for Pirkei Avot ch. 5.

Purim I

Keter Shem Tov, 207.

Purim II

Keter Shem Tov, addendum, 78.
One who reads the Megillah out
of sequence has not fulfilled his
obligation—*Megillah* 17a.

Purim III

Keter Shem Tov, addendum, 68.

Pesach

Keter Shem Tov, 154.

Shavuot

Keter Shem Tov, addendum, 14.
Vayeired... in numerous other
verses—see Genesis 38:1; Joshua 17:9,
18:16.

Pirkei Avot Ch. 1

Keter Shem Tov, 312.

Pirkei Avot Ch. 2

Keter Shem Tov, addendum, 86.

Pirkei Avot Ch. 3

Keter Shem Tov, 235.

Pirkei Avot Ch. 4

Keter Shem Tov, 171.
Af ("fury"), a name for the *yetzer
hara*—*Zohar Chadash*, Ruth, 78c.

Pirkei Avot Ch. 5

Keter Shem Tov, 188.
It was evening refers to wicked deeds,
etc.—*Midrash Rabbah*, Genesis 2:5.
[One] born under the influence of *mazal
Shabtai*...struggle[s] to concentrate—see
Shabbat 156a, and Maharsha.
Cf. teaching for Chanukah.

Pirkei Avot Ch. 6

Keter Shem Tov, 239.
A lamp in the daylight—see *Chullin* 60b.
Pleasure that comes against one's
will—*Pesachim* 25b.

Chitat[1]

Keter Shem Tov, addendum, 12.

On the Recitation of Psalms

Keter Shem Tov, addendum, *173, 10, 3, 17.*

---

1. **Editor's note:** The Tzemach Tzedek related: When I was summoned to participate in a rabbinical conference that was to take place in Petersburg, I visited the gravesite of my righteous
mother (Rebbetzin Devorah Leah) in Liozna. She told me (in a vision) that because of her self-
sacrifice on behalf of the Chassidim and (the continuation of) Chassidut she merited to enter
the (heavenly) chamber of the Baal Shem Tov in order to invoke mercy for my success.

She asked the Baal Shem Tov to provide her with some *segulah* (spiritual remedy) for me,
that I will be able to stand firm, with G-d's help, against those who oppose the ways of Chassidut. And the Baal Shem Tov answered: "Your son is after all erudite in the Five Books of the
Torah (Chumash), in Psalms (Tehillim) and in Tanya; knowing every single letter by heart.
And the verse says, 'And the terror of G-d was [upon the cities]....' The Hebrew word for 'terror'
is "*Chitat*" *(chet, tof, tof)*, which is an acronym for Chumash, Tehillim, Tanya. And one who is
erudite in their letters eradicates all challenges and concealments."

Glossary

Akeidah – The binding of our forefather Isaac (Yitzchak) by his father Abraham

Atzilut –Kabballah speaks of four spiritual worlds, the loftiest of the four being the world of *Atzilus* (followed by *Briah*)

Azarah – The Temple courtyard

Bar Mitzvah – When a Jewish boy is considered as an adult at the age of 13

Bitul – Self-nullification and/or utter devotion to God

Briah – The second of the four spiritual words (after *atzilut*)

Cheder – Jewish day school, where young children study the Torah

Chochmah – lit., intellect. The first of the 10 attributes (See *Sefirot*)

E-l - Name of God associated with kindness

Elokim – Name of God associated with concealment

Elul – The final month of the Hebrew calendar year. A month of repentance proceeding the High-Holidays

Gan Eden – The Garden of Eden, expressing the reward in the afterlife for our divine service

Hakafot – The ritual of dancing and celebrating with the Torah scrolls

Halacha – Torah law

Kabalat Ol – lit., accepting the yoke, referring to accepting the yoke and kingdom of Heaven

Kadashim Kallim – Lower-level (light) sacrifices

Ketter – The Supernal "crown." A transcendent realm of Godliness

Kodshei Kadashim – The holiest of sacrifices

Lishmah – lit., for his (God's) name, expressing concentration and devotion in Torah study, prayer and performance of *Mitzvot*

Malchut – lit., kingship. The last of the 10 attributes (See *Sefirot*)

Megillah – The Book of Ester, read on the festival of Purim

*Mitzvah (*plural: *Mitzvot) –* Divine Commandment

Rosh Hashana – The Jewish new-year (a High-Holiday)

Sefirot – The (10) Divine attributes

Selichot – Liturgy of supplication and repentance

Shachrit – The morning prayer

Shofar – a ram's horn, which we are commanded to blow on the Jewish new-year

Simchat Torah – The final day of Festivals in the month of *Tishrei*, when we dance and celebrate with the Torah scrolls (see *Hakafot*)

Sukkah – A hut we are commanded to eat in on the Festival of Sukkot

Sukkot – A Jewish festival when we are commanded to sit in a Sukkah (see Sukkah)

Teivah – lit., box. Generally referring to Noah's Ark

Teshuvah – Repentance

Tishrei – The first month of the Hebrew calendar year. A month of High-Holidays, forgiveness and Festival

Torah – The five books of Moses

Tzaddik – A truly righteous person

Yetzer hara – Evil inclination

Yetzirah – The third of the four spiritual words (after *Briah*)

Yom Kippur – The primary day of repentance and forgiveness (a High-Holiday)

Index